Among The Millet & Other Poems by Archibald Lampman

Archibald Lampman was born on November 17th 1861 at Morpeth, Ontario in Canada. Perhaps the finest Canadian Poet of his time he is classed as a Confederation Poet.

When he was 6 the family moved to Gore's Landing on Rice Lake, Ontario, where young Archie started school. In 1868 he contracted rheumatic fever, which left him lame for many years and with a permanently weakened heart.

He attended Trinity College School in Port Hope, Ontario, and then to Trinity College in Toronto, Ontario and graduated in 1882. Whilst there he published many poems in the literary journal of Victoria College.

After attempting a career as a teacher he became a clerk in the Post Office Department in Ottawa, a position he held for the rest of his life.

On Sep. 3, 1887, Arhibald married Maude Emma Playter. "They had three children; Natalie Charlotte in 1892. Arnold Gesner in May 1894, but he was only to survive a few months and in 1898 Archibald Otto, was born.

A lover of camping it inspired much of his verse and helped him to become known as 'The Canadian Keats'. Most of his poems are about the Countryside and the natural world. He wrote in excess of 300 poems and all reveal and revel in his observations of life and landscape.

But his life was destined to be cut short. His health deteriorated, due in part to the death of his second son and his earlier problems caused by rheumatic fever.

On February 10th, 1899 Archibald Lampman died of a weak heart, an after-effect of his childhood rheumatic fever in Ottawa at the age of only 37.

He is buried at Beechwood Cemetery, in Ottawa, His grave is marked by a single word on his headstone "Lampman.". A nearby plaque cites his poem "In November":
The hills grow wintry white, and bleak winds moan
About the naked uplands. I alone
Am neither sad, nor shelterless, nor gray
Wrapped round with thought, content to watch and dream.

Index Of Poems
I.   POEMS.
To My Wife
Among The Millet
April
An October Sunset
The Frogs
An Impression

Spring On The River
Why Do Ye Call The Poet Lonely
Heat
Among The Timothy
Freedom
Morning On The Lièvres
In October
Lament Of The Winds
Ballade Of Summer's Sleep
Winter
Winter Hues Recalled
Storm
Midnight
Song Of The Stream-Drops
Between The Rapids
New Year's Eve
Unrest
Song
One Day
Sleep
Three Flower Petals
Passion
A Ballade Of Waiting
Before Sleep
A Song
What Do Poets Want With Gold
The King's Sabbath
The Little Handmaiden
Abu Midjan
The Weaver
The Three Pilgrims
The Coming Of Winter
Easter Eve
The Organist
The Monk
The Child's Music Lesson
An Athenian Reverie

II.   SONNETS.
Love-Doubt
Perfect Love
Love-Wonder
Comfort
Despondency
Outlook
Gentleness
A Prayer
Music
Knowledge
Sight
An Old Lesson From The Fields

Winter-Thought
Deeds
Aspiration
The Poets
The Truth
The Martyrs
A Night Of Storm
At The Railway Station
A Forecast
In November
The City
Midsummer Night
The Loons
March
Solitude
The Maples
The Dog

I. POEMS.

To My Wife

Though fancy and the might of rhyme,
That turneth like the tide,
Have borne me many a musing time,
Beloved, from thy side,

Ah yet, I pray thee, deem not, Sweet,
Those hours were given in vain;
Within these covers to thy feet
I bring them back again.

Among The Millet

The dew is gleaming in the grass,
The morning hours are seven,
And I am fain to watch you pass,
Ye soft white clouds of heaven.

Ye stray and gather, part and fold;
The wind alone can tame you;
I think of what in time of old
The poets loved to name you.

They called you sheep, the sky your sward,
A field without a reaper;
They called the shining sun your lord,
The shepherd wind your keeper.

Your sweetest poets I will deem
The men of old for moulding
In simple beauty such a dream,
And I could lie beholding,

Where daisies in the meadow toss,
The wind from morn till even,
Forever shepherd you across
The shining field of heaven.

April

Pale season, watcher in unvexed suspense,
Still priestess of the patient middle day,
Betwixt wild March's humored petulence
And the warm wooing of green kirtled May,
Maid month of sunny peace and sober grey,
Weaver of flowers in sunward glades that ring
With murmur of libation to the spring:

As memory of pain, all past, is peace,
And joy, dream-tasted, hath the deepest cheer,
So art thou sweetest of all months that lease
The twelve short spaces of the flying year.
The bloomless days are dead, and frozen fear
No more for many moons shall vex the earth,
Dreaming of summer and fruit laden mirth.

The grey song-sparrows full of spring have sung
Their clear thin silvery tunes in leafless trees;
The robin hops, and whistles, and among
The silver-tasseled poplars the brown bees
Murmur faint dreams of summer harvestries;
The creamy sun at even scatters down
A gold-green mist across the murmuring town.

By the slow streams the frogs all day and night
Dream without thought of pain or heed of ill,
Watching the long warm silent hours take flight,
And ever with soft throats that pulse and thrill,
From the pale-weeded shallows trill and trill,
Tremulous sweet voices, flute-like, answering
One to another glorying in the spring.

All day across the ever-cloven soil,
Strong horses labour, steaming in the sun,
Down the long furrows with slow straining toil,
Turning the brown clean layers; and one by one
The crows gloom over them till daylight done
Finds them asleep somewhere in duskèd lines
Beyond the wheatlands in the northern pines.

The old year's cloaking of brown leaves that bind
The forest floor-ways, plated close and true
The last love's labour of the autumn wind
Is broken with curled flower buds white and blue
In all the matted hollows, and speared through
With thousand serpent-spotted blades up-sprung,
Yet bloomless, of the slender adder-tongue.

In the warm noon the south wind creeps and cools,
Where the red-budded stems of maples throw
Still tangled etchings on the amber pools,
Quite silent now, forgetful of the slow
Drip of the taps, the troughs, and trampled snow,
The keen March mornings, and the silvering rime
And mirthful labour of the sugar prime.

Ah, I have wandered with unwearied feet,
All the long sweetness of an April day,
Lulled with cool murmurs and the drowsy beat
Of partridge wings in secret thickets grey,
The marriage hymns of all the birds at play,
The faces of sweet flowers, and easeful dreams
Beside slow reaches of frog-haunted streams;

Wandered with happy feet, and quite forgot
The shallow toil, the strife against the grain,
Near souls, that hear us call, but answer not,
The loneliness, perplexity and pain,
And high thoughts cankered with an earthly stain
And then the long draught emptied to the lees,
I turn me homeward in slow pacing ease,

Cleaving the cedar shadows and the thin
Mist of grey gnats that cloud the river shore,
Sweet even choruses, that dance and spin
Soft tangles in the sunset; and once more
The city smites me with its dissonant roar.
To its hot heart I pass, untroubled yet,
Fed with calm hope, without desire or fret.

So to the year's first altar step I bring
Gifts of meek song, and make my spirit free
With the blind working of unanxious spring,
Careless with her, whether the days that flee
Pale drouth or golden-fruited plenty see,
So that we toil, brothers, without distress,
In calm-eyed peace and godlike blamelessness.

An October Sunset
One moment the slim cloudflakes seem to lean
With their sad sunward faces aureoled,

And longing lips set downward brightening
To take the last sweet hand kiss of the king,
Gone down beyond the closing west acold;
Paying no reverence to the slender queen,
That like a curvèd olive leaf of gold
Hangs low in heaven, rounded toward sun,
Or the small stars that one by one unfold
Down the gray border of the night begun.

The Frogs

I.

Breathers of wisdom won without a quest,
Quaint uncouth dreamers, voices high and strange,
Flutists of lands where beauty hath no change,
And wintery grief is a forgotten guest,
Sweet murmurers of everlasting rest,
For whom glad days have ever yet to run,
And moments are as æons, and the sun
But ever sunken half-way toward the west.

Often to me who heard you in your day,
With close wrapt ears, it could not choose but seem
That earth, our mother, searching in what way,
Men's hearts might know her spirit's inmost dream,
Ever at rest beneath life's change and stir,
Made you her soul, and bade you pipe for her.

II.

In those mute days when spring was in her glee,
And hope was strong, we knew not why or how,
And earth, the mother, dreamed with brooding brow.
Musing on life, and what the hours might be,
When love should ripen to maternity,
Then like high flutes in silvery interchange
Ye piped with voices still and sweet and strange,
And ever as ye piped, on every tree

The great buds swelled; among the pensive woods
The spirits of first flowers awoke and flung
From buried faces the close fitting hoods,
And listened to your piping till they fell,
The frail spring-beauty with her perfumed bell,
The wind-flower, and the spotted adder-tongue.

III.

All the day long, wherever pools might be
Among the golden meadows, where the air
Stood in a dream, as it were moorèd there
Forever in a noon-tide reverie,
Or where the birds made riot of their glee
In the still woods, and the hot sun shone down,

Crossed with warm lucent shadows on the brown
Leaf-paven pools, that bubbled dreamily,

Or far away in whispering river meads
And watery marshes where the brooding noon,
Full with the wonder of its own sweet boon,
Nestled and slept among the noiseless reeds,
Ye sat and murmured, motionless as they,
With eyes that dreamed beyond the night and day.

IV.
And when, day passed and over heaven's height,
Thin with the many stars and cool with dew,
The fingers of the deep hours slowly drew
The wonder of the ever-healing night,
No grief or loneliness or wrapt delight
Or weight of silence ever brought to you
Slumber or rest; only your voices grew
More high and solemn; slowly with hushed flight

Ye saw the echoing hours go by, long-drawn,
Nor ever stirred, watching with fathomless eyes,
And with your countless clear antiphonies
Filling the earth and heaven, even till dawn,
Last-risen, found you with its first pale gleam,
Still with soft throats unaltered in your dream.

V.
And slowly as we heard you, day by day,
The stillness of enchanted reveries
Bound brain and spirit and half-closèd eyes,
In some divine sweet wonder-dream astray;
To us no sorrow or upreared dismay
Nor any discord came, but evermore
The voices of mankind, the outer roar,
Grew strange and murmurous, faint and far away.

Morning and noon and midnight exquisitely,
Wrapt with your voices, this alone we knew,
Cities might change and fall, and men might die,
Secure were we, content to dream with you,
That change and pain are shadows faint and fleet,
And dreams are real, and life is only sweet.

An Impression
I heard the city time-bells call
Far off in hollow towers,
And one by one with measured fall
Count out the old dead hours;

I felt the march, the silent press

Of time, and held my breath;
I saw the haggard dreadfulness
Of dim old age and death.

Spring On The River

O sun, shine hot on the river;
For the ice is turning an ashen hue,
And the still bright water is looking through,
And the myriad streams are greeting you
With a ballad of life to the giver,
From forest and field and sunny town,
Meeting and running and tripping down,
With laughter and song to the river.

Oh! the din on the boats by the river;
The barges are ringing while day avails,
With sound of hewing and hammering nails,
Planing and painting and swinging pails,
All day in their shrill endeavour;
For the waters brim over their wintry cup,
And the grinding ice is breaking up,
And we must away down the river.

Oh! the hum and the toil of the river;
The ridge of the rapid sprays and skips:
Loud and low by the water's lips,
Tearing the wet pines into strips,
The saw mill is moaning ever.
The little grey sparrow skips and calls
On the rocks in the rain of the water falls,
And the logs are adrift in the river.

Oh! restlessly whirls the river;
The rivulets run and the cataract drones:
The spiders are flitting over the stones:
Summer winds float and the cedar moans;
And the eddies gleam and quiver.
O sun, shine hot, shine long and abide
In the glory and power of thy summer tide
On the swift longing face of the river.

Why Do Ye Call The Poet Lonely

Why do ye call the poet lonely,
Because he dreams in lonely places?
He is not desolate, but only
Sees, where ye cannot, hidden faces.

Heat

From plains that reel to southward, dim,

The road runs by me white and bare;
Up the steep hill it seems to swim
Beyond, and melt into the glare.
Upward half way, or it may be
Nearer the summit, slowly steals
A hay-cart, moving dustily
With idly clacking wheels.

By his cart's side the wagoner
Is slouching slowly at his ease,
Half-hidden in the windless blur
Of white dust puffing to his knees.
This wagon on the height above,
From sky to sky on either hand,
Is the sole thing that seems to move
In all the heat-held land.

Beyond me in the fields the sun
Soaks in the grass and hath his will;
I count the marguerites one by one;
Even the buttercups are still.
On the brook yonder not a breath
Disturbs the spider or the midge.
The water-bugs draw close beneath
The cool gloom of the bridge.

Where the far elm-tree shadows flood
Dark patches in the burning grass,
The cows, each with her peaceful cud,
Lie waiting for the heat to pass.
From somewhere on the slope near by
Into the pale depth of the noon
A wandering thrush slides leisurely
His thin revolving tune.

In intervals of dreams I hear
The cricket from the droughty ground;
The grass-hoppers spin into mine ear
A small innumerable sound.
I lift mine eyes sometimes to gaze:
The burning sky-line blinds my sight:
The woods far off are blue with haze;
The hills are drenched in light.

And yet to me not this or that
Is always sharp or always sweet;
In the sloped shadow of my hat
I lean at rest, and drain the heat;
Nay more, I think some blessèd power
Hath brought me wandering idly here:
In the full furnace of this hour
My thoughts grow keen and clear.

Among The Timothy

Long hours ago, while yet the morn was blithe,
Nor sharp athirst had drunk the beaded dew,
A reaper came, and swung his cradled scythe
Around this stump, and, shearing slowly, drew
Far round among the clover, ripe for hay,
A circle clean and grey;
And here among the scented swathes that gleam,
Mixed with dead daisies, it is sweet to lie
And watch the grass and the few-clouded sky,
Nor think but only dream.

For when the noon was turning, and the heat
Fell down most heavily on field and wood,
I too came hither, borne on restless feet,
Seeking some comfort for an aching mood.
Ah, I was weary of the drifting hours,
The echoing city towers,
The blind grey streets, the jingle of the throng,
Weary of hope that like a shape of stone
Sat near at hand without a smile or moan,
And weary most of song.

And those high moods of mine that sometime made
My heart a heaven, opening like a flower,
A sweeter world where I in wonder strayed,
Begirt with shapes of beauty and the power
Of dreams that moved through that enchanted clime
With changing breaths of rhyme,
Were all gone lifeless now like those white leaves,
That hang all winter, shivering dead and blind
Among the sinewy beeches in the wind,
That vainly calls and grieves.

Ah! I will set no more mine overtaskèd brain
To barren search and toil that beareth nought,
Forever following with sorefooted pain
The crossing pathways of unbournèd thought;
But let it go, as one that hath no skill,
To take what shape it will,
An ant slow-burrowing in the earthy gloom,
A spider bathing in the dew at morn,
Or a brown bee in wayward fancy borne
From hidden bloom to bloom.

Hither and thither o'er the rocking grass
The little breezes, blithe as they are blind,
Teasing the slender blossoms pass and pass,
Soft-footed children of the gipsy wind,
To taste of every purple-fringèd head

Before the bloom is dead;
And scarcely heed the daisies that, endowed
With stems so short they cannot see, up-bear
Their innocent sweet eyes distressed, and stare
Like children in a crowd.

Not far to fieldward in the central heat,
Shadowing the clover, a pale poplar stands
With glimmering leaves that, when the wind comes, beat
Together like innumerable small hands,
And with the calm, as in vague dreams astray,
Hang wan and silver-grey;
Like sleepy mænads, who in pale surprise,
Half-wakened by a prowling beast, have crept
Out of the hidden covert, where they slept,
At noon with languid eyes.

The crickets creak, and through the noonday glow,
That crazy fiddler of the hot mid-year,
The dry cicada plies his wiry bow
In long-spun cadence, thin and dusty sere:
From the green grass the small grasshoppers' din
Spreads soft and silvery thin:
And ever and anon a murmur steals
Into mine ears of toil that moves alway,
The crackling rustle of the pitch-forked hay
And lazy jerk of wheels.

As so I lie and feel the soft hours wane,
To wind and sun and peaceful sound laid bare,
That aching dim discomfort of the brain
Fades off unseen, and shadowy-footed care
Into some hidden corner creeps at last
To slumber deep and fast;
And gliding on, quite fashioned to forget,
From dream to dream I bid my spirit pass
Out into the pale green ever-swaying grass
To brood, but no more fret.

And hour by hour among all shapes that grow
Of purple mints and daisies gemmed with gold
In sweet unrest my visions come and go;
I feel and hear and with quiet eyes behold;
And hour by hour, the ever-journeying sun,
In gold and shadow spun,
Into mine eyes and blood, and through the dim
Green glimmering forest of the grass shines down,
Till flower and blade, and every cranny brown,
And I are soaked with him.

Freedom

Out of the heart of the city begotten
Of the labour of men and their manifold hands,
Whose souls, that were sprung from the earth in her morning,
No longer regard or remember her warning,
Whose hearts in the furnace of care have forgotten
Forever the scent and the hue of her lands;

Out of the heat of the usurer's hold,
From the horrible crash of the strong man's feet;
Out of the shadow where pity is dying;
Out of the clamour where beauty is lying,
Dead in the depth of the struggle for gold;
Out of the din and the glare of the street;

Into the arms of our mother we come,
Our broad strong mother, the innocent earth,
Mother of all things beautiful, blameless,
Mother of hopes that her strength makes tameless,
Where the voices of grief and of battle are dumb,
And the whole world laughs with the light of her mirth.

Over the fields, where the cool winds sweep,
Black with the mould and brown with the loam,
Where the thin green spears of the wheat are appearing,
And the high-ho shouts from the smoky clearing;
Over the widths where the cloud shadows creep;
Over the fields and the fallows we come;

Over the swamps with their pensive noises,
Where the burnished cup of the marigold gleams;
Skirting the reeds, where the quick winds shiver
On the swelling breast of the dimpled river,
And the blue of the king-fisher hangs and poises,
Watching a spot by the edge of the streams;

By the miles of the fences warped and dyed
With the white-hot noons and their withering fires,
Where the rough bees trample the creamy bosoms
Of the hanging tufts of the elder blossoms,
And the spiders weave, and the grey snakes hide,
In the crannied gloom of the stones and the briers;

Over the meadow lands sprouting with thistle,
Where the humming wings of the blackbirds pass,
Where the hollows are banked with the violets flowering,
And the long-limbed pendulous elms are towering,
Where the robins are loud with their voluble whistle,
And the ground sparrow scurries away through the grass,

Where the restless bobolink loiters and woos
Down in the hollows and over the swells,
Dropping in and out of the shadows,

Sprinkling his music about the meadows,
Whistles and little checks and coos,
And the tinkle of glassy bells;

Into the dim woods full of the tombs
Of the dead trees soft in their sepulchres,
Where the pensive throats of the shy birds hidden,
Pipe to us strangely entering unbidden,
And tenderly still in the tremulous glooms
The trilliums scatter their white-winged stars;

Up to the hills where our tired hearts rest,
Loosen, and halt, and regather their dreams;
Up to the hills, where the winds restore us,
Clearing our eyes to the beauty before us,
Earth with the glory of life on her breast,
Earth with the gleam of her cities and streams.

Here we shall commune with her and no other;
Care and the battle of life shall cease;
Men her degenerate children behind us,
Only the might of her beauty shall bind us,
Full of rest, as we gaze on the face of our mother,
Earth in the health and the strength of her peace.

Morning On The Lievres
Far above us where a jay
Screams his matins to the day,
Capped with gold and amethyst,
Like a vapour from the forge
Of a giant somewhere hid,
Out of hearing of the clang
Of his hammer, skirts of mist
Slowly up the woody gorge
Lift and hang.

Softly as a cloud we go,
Sky above and sky below,
Down the river, and the dip
Of the paddles scarcely breaks,
With the little silvery drip
Of the water as it shakes
From the blades, the crystal deep
Of the silence of the morn,
Of the forest yet asleep,
And the river reaches borne
In a mirror, purple grey,
Sheer away
To the misty line of light,
Where the forest and the stream
In the shadow meet and plight,

Like a dream.

From amid a stretch of reeds,
Where the lazy river sucks
All the water as it bleeds
From a little curling creek,
And the muskrats peer and sneak
In around the sunken wrecks
Of a tree that swept the skies
Long ago,
On a sudden seven ducks
With a splashy rustle rise,
Stretching out their seven necks,
One before, and two behind,
And the others all arow,
And as steady as the wind
With a swivelling whistle go,
Through the purple shadow led,
Till we only hear their whir
In behind a rocky spur,
Just ahead.

In October

Along the waste, a great way off, the pines,
Like tall slim priests of storm, stand up and bar
The low long strip of dolorous red that lines
The under west, where wet winds moan afar.
The cornfields all are brown, and brown the meadows
With the blown leaves' wind-heapèd traceries,
And the brown thistle stems that cast no shadows,
And bear no bloom for bees.

As slowly earthward leaf by red leaf slips,
The sad trees rustle in chill misery,
A soft strange inner sound of pain-crazed lips,
That move and murmur incoherently;
As if all leaves, that yet have breath, were sighing,
With pale hushed throats, for death is at the door,
So many low soft masses for the dying
Sweet leaves that live no more.

Here I will sit upon this naked stone,
Draw my coat closer with my numbèd hands,
And hear the ferns sigh, and the wet woods moan,
And send my heart out to the ashen lands;
And I will ask myself what golden madness,
What balmèd breaths of dreamland spicery,
What visions of soft laughter and light sadness
Were sweet last month to me.

The dry dead leaves flit by with thin wierd tunes,

Like failing murmurs of some conquered creed,
Graven in mystic markings with strange runes,
That none but stars and biting winds may read;
Here I will wait a little; I am weary,
Not torn with pain of any lurid hue,
But only still and very gray and dreary,
Sweet sombre lands, like you.

Lament Of The Winds
We in sorrow coldly witting,
In the bleak world sitting, sitting,
By the forest, near the mould,
Heard the summer calling, calling,
Through the dead leaves falling, falling,
That her life grew faint and old.

And we took her up, and bore her,
With the leaves that moaned before her,
To the holy forest bowers,
Where the trees were dense and serried,
And her corpse we buried, buried,
In the graveyard of the flowers.

Now the leaves, as death grows vaster,
Yellowing deeper, dropping faster,
All the grave wherein she lies
With their bodies cover, cover,
With their hearts that love her, love her,
For they live not when she dies:

And we left her so, but stay not
Of our tears, and yet we may not,
Though they coldly thickly fall,
Give the dead leaves any, any,
For they lie so many, many,
That we cannot weep for all.

Ballade Of Summer's Sleep
Sweet summer is gone; they have laid her away
The last sad hours that were touched with her grace
In the hush where the ghosts of the dead flowers play;
The sleep that is sweet of her slumbering space
Let not a sight or a sound erase
Of the woe that hath fallen on all the lands:
Gather ye, dreams, to her sunny face,
Shadow her head with your golden hands.

The woods that are golden and red for a day
Girdle the hills in a jewelled case,
Like a girl's strange mirth, ere the quick death slay

The beautiful life that he hath in chase.
Darker and darker the shadows pace
Out of the north to the southern sands,
Ushers bearing the winter's mace:
Keep them away with your woven hands.

The yellow light lies on the wide wastes gray,
More bitter and cold than the winds that race,
From the skirts of the autumn, tearing away,
This way and that way, the woodland lace.
In the autumn's cheek is a hectic trace;
Behind her the ghost of the winter stands;
Sweet summer will moan in her soft gray place:
Mantle her head with your glowing hands.

Envoi.
Till the slayer be slain and the spring displace
The might of his arms with her rose-crowned bands,
Let her heart not gather a dream that is base:
Shadow her head with your golden hands.

Winter

The long days came and went; the riotous bees
Tore the warm grapes in many a dusty-vine,
And men grew faint and thin with too much ease,
And Winter gave no sign:
But all the while beyond the northmost woods
He sat and smiled and watched his spirits play
In elfish dance and eery roundelay,
Tripping in many moods
With snowy curve and fairy crystal shine.

But now the time is come: with southward speed
The elfin spirits pass: a secret sting
Hath fallen and smitten flower and fruit and weed,
And every leafy thing.
The wet woods moan: the dead leaves break and fall;
In still night-watches wakeful men have heard
The muffled pipe of many a passing bird,
High over hut and hall,
Straining to southward with unresting wing.

And then they come with colder feet, and fret
The winds with snow, and tuck the streams to sleep
With icy sheet and gleaming coverlet,
And fill the valleys deep
With curvèd drifts, and a strange music raves
Among the pines, sometimes in wails, and then
In whistled laughter, till affrighted men
Draw close, and into caves
And earthy holes the blind beasts curl and creep.

And so all day above the toiling heads
Of men's poor chimneys, full of impish freaks,
Tearing and twisting in tight-curlèd shreds
The vain unnumbered reeks,
The Winter speeds his fairies forth and mocks
Poor bitten men with laughter icy cold,
Turning the brown of youth to white and old
With hoary-woven locks,
And grey men young with roses in their cheeks.

And after thaws, when liberal water swells
The bursting eaves, he biddeth drip and grow
The curly horns of ribbèd icicles
In many a beard-like row.
In secret moods of mercy and soft dole,
Old warpèd wrecks and things of mouldering death
That summer scorns and man abandoneth
His careful hands console
With lawny robes and draperies of snow.

And when night comes, his spirits with chill feet,
Winged with white mirth and noiseless mockery,
Across men's pallid windows peer and fleet,
And smiling silverly
Draw with mute fingers on the frosted glass
Quaint fairy shapes of icèd witcheries,
Pale flowers and glinting ferns and frigid trees
And meads of mystic grass,
Graven in many an austere phantasy.

But far away the Winter dreams alone,
Rustling among his snow-drifts, and resigns
Cold fondling ears to hear the cedars moan
In dusky-skirted lines
Strange answers of an ancient runic call;
Or somewhere watches with his antique eyes,
Gray-chill with frosty-lidded reveries,
The silvery moonshine fall
In misty wedges through his girth of pines.

Poor mortals haste and hide away: creep soon
Into your icy beds: the embers die;
And on your frosted panes the pallid moon
Is glimmering brokenly.
Mutter faint prayers that spring will come e'erwhile,
Scarring with thaws and dripping days and nights
The shining majesty of him that smites
And slays you with a smile
Upon his silvery lips, of glinting mockery.

Winter Hues Recalled

Life is not all for effort: there are hours,
When fancy breaks from the exacting will,
And rebel thought takes schoolboy's holiday,
Rejoicing in its idle strength. 'Tis then,
And only at such moments, that we know
The treasure of hours gone - scenes once beheld,
Sweet voices and words bright and beautiful,
Impetuous deeds that woke the God within us,
The loveliness of forms and thoughts and colors,
A moment marked and then as soon forgotten.
These things are ever near us, laid away,
Hidden and waiting the appropriate times,
In the quiet garner-house of memory.
There in the silent unaccounted depth,
Beneath the heated strainage and the rush
That teem the noisy surface of the hours,
All things that ever touched us are stored up,
Growing more mellow like sealed wine with age;
We thought them dead, and they are but asleep.
In moments when the heart is most at rest
And least expectant, from the luminous doors,
And sacred dwelling place of things unfeared,
They issue forth, and we who never knew
Till then how potent and how real they were,
Take them, and wonder, and so bless the hour.

Such gifts are sweetest when unsought. To me,
As I was loitering lately in my dreams,
Passing from one remembrance to another,
Like him who reads upon an outstretched map,
Content and idly happy, these rose up,
Out of that magic well-stored picture house,
No dream, rather a thing most keenly real,
The memory of a moment, when with feet,
Arrested and spell bound, and captured eyes,
Made wide with joy and wonder, I beheld
The spaces of a white and wintery land
Swept with the fire of sunset, all its width
Vale, forest, town, and misty eminence,
A miracle of color and of beauty.

I had walked out, as I remember now,
With covered ears, for the bright air was keen,
To southward up the gleaming snow-packed fields,
With the snowshoer's long rejoicing stride,
Marching at ease. It was a radiant day
In February, the month of the great struggle
'Twixt sun and frost, when with advancing spears,
The glittering golden vanguard of the spring
Holds the broad winter's yet unbroken rear
In long-closed wavering contest. Thin pale threads

Like streaks of ash across the far off blue
Were drawn, nor seemed to move. A brooding silence
Kept all the land, a stillness as of sleep;
But in the east the grey and motionless woods,
Watching the great sun's fiery slow decline,
Grew deep with gold. To westward all was silver.
An hour had passed above me; I had reached
The loftiest level of the snow-piled fields,
Clear eyed, but unobservant, noting not,
That all the plain beneath me and the hills
Took on a change of color splendid, gradual,
Leaving no spot the same; nor that the sun
Now like a fiery torrent overflamed
The great line of the west. Ere yet I turned
With long stride homeward, being heated
With the loose swinging motion, weary too,
Nor uninclined to rest, a buried fence,
Whose topmost log just shouldered from the snow,
Made me a seat, and thence with heated cheeks,
Grazed by the northwind's edge of stinging ice,
I looked far out upon the snow-bound waste,
The lifting hills and intersecting forests,
The scarce marked courses of the buried streams,
And as I looked lost memory of the frost,
Transfixed with wonder, overborne with joy.
I saw them in their silence and their beauty,
Swept by the sunset's rapid hand of fire,
Sudden, mysterious, every moment deepening
To some new majesty of rose or flame.
The whole broad west was like a molten sea
Of crimson. In the north the light-lined hills
Were veiled far off as with a mist of rose
Wondrous and soft. Along the darkening east
The gold of all the forests slowly changed
To purple. In the valley far before me,
Low sunk in sapphire shadows, from its hills,
Softer and lovelier than an opening flower,
Uprose a city with its sun-touched towers,
A bunch of amethysts.
Like one spell-bound
Caught in the presence of some god, I stood,
Nor felt the keen wind and the deadly air,
But watched the sun go down, and watched the gold
Fade from the town and the withdrawing hills,
Their westward shapes athwart the dusky red
Freeze into sapphire, saw the arc of rose
Rise ever higher in the violet east,
Above the frore front of the uprearing night
Remorsefully soft and sweet. Then I awoke
As from a dream, and from my shoulders shook
The warning chill, till then unfelt, unfeared.

Storm

Out of the grey northwest, where many a day gone by
Ye tugged and howled in your tempestuous grot,
And evermore the huge frost giants lie,
Your wizard guards in vigilance unforgot,
Out of the grey northwest, for now the bonds are riven,
On wide white wings your thongless flight is driven,
That lulls but resteth not.

And all the grey day long, and all the dense wild night
Ye wheel and hurry with the sheeted snow,
By cedared waste and many a pine-dark height,
Across white rivers frozen fast below;
Over the lonely forests, where the flowers yet sleeping
Turn in their narrow beds with dreams of weeping
In some remembered woe;

Across the unfenced wide marsh levels, where the dry
Brown ferns sigh out, and last year's sedges scold
In some drear language, rustling haggardly
Their thin dead leaves and dusky hoods of gold;
Across grey beechwoods where the pallid leaves unfalling
In the blind gusts like homeless ghosts are calling
With voices cracked and old;

Across the solitary clearings, where the low
Fierce gusts howl through the blinded woods, and round
The buried shanties all day long the snow
Sifts and piles up in many a spectral mound;
Across lone villages in eery wildernesses
Whose hidden life no living shape confesses
Nor any human sound;

Across the serried masses of dim cities, blown
Full of the snow that ever shifts and swells,
While far above them all their towers of stone
Stand and beat back your fierce and tyrannous spells,
And hour by hour send out, like voices torn and broken
Of battling giants that have grandly spoken,
The veering sound of bells;

So day and night, oh wind, with hiss and moan you fleet,
Where once long gone on many a green-leafed day
Your gentler brethren wandered with light feet
And sang with voices soft and sweet as they,
The same blind thought that you with wilder might are speaking,
Seeking the same strange thing that you are seeking
In this your stormier way.

Oh wind, wild-voicèd brother, in your northern cave,
My spirit also being so beset

With pride and pain, I heard you beat and rave,
Grinding your chains with furious howl and fret,
Knowing full well that all earth's moving things inherit
The same chained might and madness of the spirit,
That none may quite forget.

You in your cave of snows, we in our narrow girth
Of need and sense, forever chafe and pine;
Only in moods of some demonic birth
Our souls take fire, our flashing wings untwine;
Even like you, mad wind, above our broken prison,
With streaming hair and maddened eyes uprisen,
We dream ourselves divine;

Mad moods that come and go in some mysterious way,
That flash and fall, none knoweth how or why,
Oh wind, our brother, they are yours to-day,
The stormy joy, the sweeping mastery;
Deep in our narrow cells, we hear you, we awaken
With hands afret and bosoms strangely shaken,
We answer to your cry.

I most that love you, wind, when you are fierce and free,
In these dull fetters cannot long remain;
Lo, I will rise and break my thongs and flee
Forth to your drift and beating, till my brain
Even for an hour grow wild in your divine embraces,
And then creep back into mine earthly traces,
And bind me with my chain.

Nay, wind, I hear you, desperate brother, in your might
Whistle and howl; I shall not tarry long,
And though the day be blind and fierce, the night
Be dense and wild, I still am glad and strong
To meet you face to face; through all your gust and drifting
With brow held high, my joyous hands uplifting,
I cry you song for song.

Midnight
From where I sit, I see the stars,
And down the chilly floor
The moon between the frozen bars
Is glimmering dim and hoar.

Without in many a peakèd mound
The glinting snowdrifts lie;
There is no voice or living sound;
The embers slowly die.

Yet some wild thing is in mine ear;
I hold my breath and hark;

Out of the depth I seem to hear
A crying in the dark:

No sound of man or wife or child,
No sound of beast that groans,
Or of the wind that whistles wild,
Or of the tree that moans:

I know not what it is I hear;
I bend my head and hark:
I cannot drive it from mine ear,
That crying in the dark.

Song Of The Steam-Drops

By silent forest and field and mossy stone,
We come from the wooded hill, and we go to the sea.
We labour, and sing sweet songs, but we never moan,
For our mother, the sea, is calling us cheerily.
We have heard her calling us many and many a day
From the cool grey stones and the white sands far away.

The way is long, and winding and slow is the track,
The sharp rocks fret us, the eddies bring us delay,
But we sing sweet songs to our mother, and answer her back;
Gladly we answer our mother, sweetly repay.
Oh, we hear, we hear her singing wherever we roam,
Far, far away in the silence, calling us home.

Poor mortal, your ears are dull, and you cannot hear;
But we, we hear it, the breast of our mother abeat;
Low, far away, sweet and solemn and clear,
Under the hush of the night, under the noontide heat:
And we sing sweet songs to our mother, for so we shall please her best,
Songs of beauty and peace, freedom and infinite rest.

We sing, and sing, through the grass and the stones and the reeds,
And we never grow tired, though we journey ever and aye,
Dreaming, and dreaming, wherever the long way leads,
Of the far cool rocks and the rush of the wind and the spray.
Under the sun and the stars we murmur and dance and are free,
And we dream and dream of our mother, the width of the sheltering sea.

Between The Rapids

The point is turned; the twilight shadow fills
The wheeling stream, the soft receding shore,
And on our ears from deep among the hills
Breaks now the rapid's sudden quickening roar.
Ah yet the same, or have they changed their face,
The fair green fields, and can it still be seen,
The white log cottage near the mountain's base,

So bright and quiet, so home-like and serene?
Ah, well I question, for as five years go,
How many blessings fall, and how much woe.

Aye there they are, nor have they changed their cheer,
The fields, the hut, the leafy mountain brows;
Across the lonely dusk again I hear
The loitering bells, the lowing of the cows,
The bleat of many sheep, the stilly rush
Of the low whispering river, and through all,
Soft human tongues that break the deepening hush
With faint-heard song or desultory call:
Oh comrades hold; the longest reach is past;
The stream runs swift, and we are flying fast.

The shore, the fields, the cottage just the same,
But how with them whose memory makes them sweet?
Oh if I called them, hailing name by name,
Would the same lips the same old shouts repeat?
Have the rough years, so big with death and ill,
Gone lightly by and left them smiling yet?
Wild black-eyed Jeanne whose tongue was never still,
Old wrinkled Picaud, Pierre and pale Lisette,
The homely hearts that never cared to range,
While life's wide fields were filled with rush and change.

And where is Jacques, and where is Verginie?
I cannot tell; the fields are all a blur.
The lowing cows whose shapes I scarcely see,
Oh do they wait and do they call for her?
And is she changed, or is her heart still clear
As wind or morning, light as river foam?
Or have life's changes borne her far from here,
And far from rest, and far from help and home?
Ah comrades, soft, and let us rest awhile,
For arms grow tired with paddling many a mile.

The woods grow wild, and from the rising shore
The cool wind creeps, the faint wood odours steal;
Like ghosts adown the river's blackening floor
The misty fumes begin to creep and reel.
Once more I leave you, wandering toward the night,
Sweet home, sweet heart, that would have held me in;
Whither I go I know not, and the light
Is faint before, and rest is hard to win.
Ah sweet ye were and near to heaven's gate;
But youth is blind and wisdom comes too late.

Blacker and loftier grow the woods, and hark!
The freshening roar! The chute is near us now,
And dim the canyon grows, and inky dark
The water whispering from the birchen prow.

One long last look, and many a sad adieu,
While eyes can see and heart can feel you yet,
I leave sweet home and sweeter hearts to you,
A prayer for Picaud, one for pale Lisette,
A kiss for Pierre, my little Jacques, and thee,
A sigh for Jeanne, a sob for Verginie.

Oh, does she still remember? Is the dream
Now dead, or has she found another mate?
So near, so dear; and ah, so swift the stream;
Even now perhaps it were not yet too late.
But oh, what matter; for before the night
Has reached its middle, we have far to go:
Bend to your paddles, comrades; see, the light
Ebbs off apace; we must not linger so.
Aye thus it is! Heaven gleams and then is gone
Once, twice, it smiles, and still we wander on.

New Year's Eve
Once on the year's last eve in my mind's might
Sitting in dreams, not sad, nor quite elysian,
Balancing all 'twixt wonder and derision,
Methought my body and all this world took flight,
And vanished from me, as a dream, outright;
Leaning out thus in sudden strange decision,
I saw as it were in the flashing of a vision,
Far down between the tall towers of the night,
Borne by great winds in awful unison,
The teeming masses of mankind sweep by,
Even as a glittering river with deep sound
And innumerable banners, rolling on
Over the starry border glooms that bound
The last gray space in dim eternity.

And all that strange unearthly multitude
Seemed twisted in vast seething companies,
That evermore with hoarse and terrible cries
And desperate encounter at mad feud
Plunged onward, each in its implacable mood
Borne down over the trampled blazonries
Of other faiths and other phantasies,
Each following furiously, and each pursued;
So sped they on with tumult vast and grim,
But ever meseemed beyond them I could see
White-haloed groups that sought perpetually
The figure of one crowned and sacrificed;
And faint, far forward, floating tall and dim,
The banner of our Lord and Master, Christ.

Unrest

All day upon the garden bright
The sun shines strong,
But in my heart there is no light,
Or any song.

Voices of merry life go by,
Adown the street;
But I am weary of the cry
And drift of feet.

With all dear things that ought to please
The hours are blessed,
And yet my soul is ill at ease,
And cannot rest.

Strange spirit, leave me not too long,
Nor stint to give,
For if my soul have no sweet song,
It cannot live.

Song

Songs that could span the earth,
When leaping thought had stirred them,
In many an hour since birth,
We heard or dreamed we heard them.

Sometimes to all their sway
We yield ourselves half fearing,
Sometimes with hearts grown grey
We curse ourselves for hearing.

We toil and but begin;
In vain our spirits fret them,
We strive, and cannot win,
Nor evermore forget them.

A light that will not stand,
That comes and goes in flashes,
Fair fruits that in the hand
Are turned to dust and ashes.

Yet still the deep thoughts ring
Around and through and through us,
Sweet mights that make us sing,
But bring no resting to us.

One Day

The trees rustle; the wind blows
Merrily out of the town;
The shadows creep, the sun goes

Steadily over and down.

In a brown gloom the moats gleam;
Slender the sweet wife stands;
Her lips are red; her eyes dream;
Kisses are warm on her hands.

The child moans; the hours slip
Bitterly over her head:
In a gray dusk, the tears drip;
Mother is up there dead.

The hermit hears the strange bright
Murmur of life at play;
In the waste day and the waste night
Times to rebel and to pray.

The laborer toils in gray wise,
Godlike and patient and calm;
The beggar moans; his bleared eyes
Measure the dust in his palm.

The wise man marks the flow and ebb
Hidden and held aloof:
In his deep mind is laid the web,
Shuttles are driving the woof.

Sleep

If any man, with sleepless care oppressed,
On many a night had risen, and addressed
His hand to make him out of joy and moan
An image of sweet sleep in carven stone,
Light touch by touch, in weary moments planned,
He would have wrought her with a patient hand,
Not like her brother death, with massive limb
And dreamless brow, unstartled, changeless, dim,
But very fair, though fitful and afraid,
More sweet and slight than any mortal maid.
Her hair he would have carved a mantle smooth
Down to her tender feet to wrap and soothe
All fevers in, yet barbèd here and there
With many a hidden sting of restless care;
Her brow most quiet, thick with opiate rest,
Yet watchfully lined, as if some hovering guest
Of noiseless doubt were there; so too her eyes
His light hand would have carved in cunning wise
Broad with all languor of the drowsy South,
Most beautiful, but held askance; her mouth
More soft and round than any rose half-spread,
Yet ever twisted with some nervous dread.
He would have made her with one marble foot,

Frail as a snow-white feather, forward put,
Bearing sweet medicine for all distress,
Smooth languor and unstrung forgetfulness;
The other held a little back for dread;
One slender moonpale hand held forth to shed
Soft slumber dripping from its pearly tip
Into wide eyes; the other on her lip.
So in the watches of his sleepless care
The cunning artist would have wrought her fair;
Shy goddess, at keen seeking most afraid
Yet often coming, when we least have prayed.

Three Flower Petals

What saw I yesterday walking apart
In a leafy place where the cattle wait?
Something to keep for a charm in my heart
A little sweet girl in a garden gate.
Laughing she lay in the gold sun's might,
And held for a target to shelter her,
In her little soft fingers, round and white,
The gold-rimmed face of a sunflower.

Laughing she lay on the stone that stands
For a rough-hewn step in that sunny place,
And her yellow hair hung down to her hands,
Shadowing over her dimpled face.
Her eyes like the blue of the sky, made dim
With the might of the sun that looked at her,
Shone laughing over the serried rim,
Golden set, of the sunflower.

Laughing, for token she gave to me
Three petals out of the sunflower;
When the petals are withered and gone, shall be
Three verses of mine for praise of her,
That a tender dream of her face may rise
And lighten me yet in another hour,
Of her sunny hair and her beautiful eyes,
Laughing over the gold sunflower.

Passion

As a weed beneath the ocean,
As a pool beneath a tree
Answers with each breath or motion
An imperious mastery;

So my spirit swift with passion
Finds in every look a sign,
Catching in some wondrous fashion
Every mood that governs thine.

In a moment it will borrow,
Flashing in a gusty train,
Laughter and desire and sorrow
Anger and delight and pain.

A Ballade Of Waiting

No girdle hath weaver or goldsmith wrought
So rich as the arms of my love can be;
No gems with a lovelier lustre fraught
Than her eyes, when they answer me liquidly.
Dear lady of love, be kind to me
In days when the waters of hope abate,
And doubt like a shimmer on sand shall be,
In the year yet, Lady, to dream and wait.

Sweet mouth, that the wear of the world hath taught
No glitter of wile or traitorie,
More soft than a cloud in the sunset caught,
Or the heart of a crimson peony;
Oh turn not its beauty away from me;
To kiss it and cling to it early and late
Shall make sweet minutes of days that flee,
In the year yet, Lady, to dream and wait.

Rich hair that a painter of old had sought
For the weaving of some soft phantasy,
Most fair when the streams of it run distraught
On the firm sweet shoulders yellowly;
Dear Lady, gather it close to me,
Weaving a nest for the double freight
Of cheeks and lips that are one and free,
For the year yet, Lady, to dream and wait.

Envoi.
So time shall be swift till thou mate with me,
For love is mightiest next to fate,
And none shall be happier, Love, than we,
In the year yet, Lady, to dream and wait.

Before Sleep

Now the creeping nets of sleep
Stretch about and gather nigh,
And the midnight dim and deep
Like a spirit passes by,
Trailing from her crystal dress
Dreams and silent frostiness.

Yet a moment, ere I be
Tangled in the snares of night,

All the dreamy heart of me
To my Lady takes its flight,
To her chamber where she lies,
Wrapt in midnight phantasies.

Over many a glinting street
And the snow capped roofs of men,
Towers that tremble with the beat
Of the midnight bells, and then,
Where my body may not be,
Stands my spirit holily.

Wake not, Lady, wake not soon:
Through the frosty windows fall
Broken glimmers of the moon
Dimly on the floor and wall;
Wake not, Lady, never care,
'Tis my spirit kneeling there.

Let him kneel a moment now,
For the minutes fly apace;
Let him see the sleeping brow,
And the sweetly rounded face:
He shall tell me soon aright
How my Lady looks to-night.

How her tresses out and in
Fold in many a curly freak,
Round about the snowy chin
And the softly tinted cheek,
Where no sorrows now can weep,
And the dimples lie asleep.

How her eyelids meet and match,
Gathered in two dusky seams,
Each the little creamy thatch
Of an azure house of dreams,
Or two flowers that love the light
Folded softly up at night.

How her bosom, breathing low,
Stirs the wavy coverlet
With a motion soft and slow:
Oh, my Lady, wake not yet;
There without a thought of guile
Let my spirit dream a while.

Yet, my spirit, back to me,
Hurry soon and have a care;
Love will turn to agony,
If you rashly linger there;
Bending low as spirits may,

Touch her lips and come away.

So, fond spirit, beauty-fed,
Turning when your watch is o'er,
Weave a cross above the bed
And a sleep-rune on the floor,
That no evil enter there,
Ugly shapes and dreams beware.

Then, ye looming nets of sleep,
Ye may have me all your own,
For the night is wearing deep
And the ice-winds whisk and moan;
Come with all your drowsy stress,
Dreams and silent frostiness.

A Song
Oh night and sleep,
Ye are so soft and deep,
I am so weary, come ye soon to me.
Oh hours that creep,
With so much time to weep,
I am so tired, can ye no swifter be?

Come, night, anear;
I'll whisper in thine ear
What makes me so unhappy, full of care;
Dear night, I die
For love that all men buy
With tears, and know not it is dark despair.

Dear night, I pray,
How is it that men say
That love is sweet? It is not sweet to me.
For one boy's sake
A poor girl's heart must break;
So sweet, so true, and yet it could not be!

Oh, I loved well,
Such love as none can tell:
It was so true, it could not make him know:
For he was blind,
All light and all unkind:
Oh, had he known, would he have hurt me so?

Oh night and sleep,
Ye are so soft and deep,
I am so weary, come ye soon to me.
Oh hours that creep,
With so much time to weep,
I am so tired, can ye no swifter be?

What Do Poets Want With Gold?

What do poets want with gold,
Cringing slaves and cushioned ease;
Are not crusts and garments old
Better for their souls than these?

Gold is but the juggling rod
Of a false usurping god,
Graven long ago in hell
With a sombre stony spell,
Working in the world forever.
Hate is not so strong to sever
Beating human heart from heart.
Soul from soul we shrink and part,
And no longer hail each other
With the ancient name of brother
Give the simple poet gold,
And his song will die of cold.
He must walk with men that reel
On the rugged path, and feel
Every sacred soul that is
Beating very near to his.
Simple, human, careless, free,
As God made him, he must be:
For the sweetest song of bird
Is the hidden tenor heard
In the dusk, at even-flush,
From the forest's inner hush,
Of the simple hermit thrush.

What do poets want with love?
Flowers that shiver out of hand,
And the fervid fruits that prove
Only bitter broken sand?

Poets speak of passion best,
When their dreams are undistressed,
And the sweetest songs are sung,
E'er the inner heart is stung.
Let them dream; 'tis better so;
Ever dream, but never know.
If their spirits once have drained
All that goblet crimson-stained,
Finding what they dreamed divine,
Only earthly sluggish wine,
Sooner will the warm lips pale,
And the flawless voices fail,
Sooner come the drooping wing,
And the afterdays that bring,
No such songs as did the spring.

The King's Sabbath

Once idly in his hall king Olave sat
Pondering, and with his dagger whittled chips;
And one drew near to him with austere lips,
Saying, "To-morrow is Monday," and at that
The king said nothing, but held forth his flat
Broad palm, and bending on his mighty hips,
Took up and mutely laid thereon the slips
Of scattered wood, as on a hearth, and gat
From off the embers near, a burning brand.
Kindling the pile with this, the dreaming Dane
Sat silent with his eyes set and his bland
Proud mouth, tight-woven, smiling, drawn with pain,
Watching the fierce fire flare, and wax, and wane,
Hiss and burn down upon his shrivelled hand.

The Little Handmaiden

The King's son walks in the garden fair
Oh, the maiden's heart is merry!
He little knows for his toil and care,
That the bride is gone and the bower is bare.
Put on garments of white, my maidens!

The sun shines bright through the casement high
Oh, the maiden's heart is merry!
The little handmaid, with a laughing eye,
Looks down on the king's son, strolling by.
Put on garments of white, my maidens!

"He little knows that the bride is gone,
And the Earl knows little as he;
She is fled with her lover afar last night,
And the King's son is left to me."

And back to her chamber with velvety step
The little handmaid did glide,
And a gold key took from her bosom sweet,
And opened the great chests wide.

She bound her hair with a band of blue,
And a garland of lilies sweet;
And put on her delicate silken shoes,
With roses on both her feet.

She clad her body in spotless white,
With a girdle as red as blood.
The glad white raiment her beauty bound,
As the sepels bind the bud:

And round and round her white neck she flung
A necklace of sapphires blue;
On one white finger of either hand
A shining ring she drew.

And down the stairway and out of the door
She glided, as soft and light,
As an airy tuft of a thistle seed
Might glide through the grasses bright.

And into the garden sweet she stole
The little birds carolled loud
Her beauty shone as a star might shine
In the rift of a morning cloud.

The King's son walked in the garden fair,
And the little handmaiden came,
Through the midst of a shimmer of roses red,
Like a sunbeam through a flame.

The King's son marvelled, his heart leaped up,
"And art thou my bride?" said he,
"For, North or South, I have never beheld
A lovelier maid than thee."

"And dost thou love me?" the little maid cried,
"A fine King's son, I wis!"
And the King's son took her with both his hands,
And her ruddy lips did kiss.

And the little maid laughed till the beaded tears,
Ran down in a silver rain.
"O foolish King's son!" and she clapped her hands,
Till the gold rings rang again.

"O King's son, foolish and fooled art thou,
For a goodly game is played:
Thy bride is away with her lover last night,
And I am her little handmaid."

And the King's son sware a great oath, said he,
Oh, the maiden's heart is merry!
"If the Earl's fair daughter a traitress be,
The little handmaid is enough for me."
Put on garments of white, my maidens!

The King's son walks in the garden fair
Oh, the maiden's heart is merry!
And the little handmaiden walketh there,
But the old Earl pulleth his beard for care.
Put on garments of white, my maidens!

Abu Midjan

Underneath a tree at noontide
Abu Midjan sits distressed,
Fetters on his wrists and ankles,
And his chin upon his breast;

For the Emir's guard had taken,
As they passed from line to line,
Reeling in the camp at midnight,
Abu Midjan drunk with wine.

Now he sits and rolls uneasy,
Very fretful, for he hears,
Near at hand, the shout of battle,
And the din of driving spears.

Both his heels in wrath are digging
Trenches in the grassy soil,
And his fingers clutch and loosen,
Dreaming of the Persian spoil.

To the garden, over-weary
Of the sound of hoof and sword,
Came the Emir's gentle lady,
Anxious for her fighting lord.

Very sadly, Abu Midjan,
Hanging down his head for shame,
Spake in words of soft appealing
To the tender-hearted dame:

"Lady, while the doubtful battle
Ebbs and flows upon the plains,
Here in sorrow, meek and idle,
Abu Midjan sits in chains.

"Surely Saad would be safer
For the strength of even me;
Give me then his armour, Lady,
And his horse, and set me free.

"When the day of fight is over,
With the spoil that he may earn,
To his chains, if he is living,
Abu Midjan will return."

She, in wonder and compassion,
Had not heart to say him nay;
So, with Saad's horse and armour,
Abu Midjan rode away.

Happy from the fight at even,
Saad told his wife at meat,
How the army had been succoured
In the fiercest battle-heat,

By a stranger horseman, coming
When their hands were most in need,
And he bore the arms of Saad,
And was mounted on his steed;

How the faithful battled forward,
Mighty where the stranger trod,
Till they deemed him more than mortal,
And an angel sent from God.

Then the lady told her master
How she gave the horse and mail
To the drunkard, and had taken
Abu Midjan's word for bail.

To the garden went the Emir,
Running to the tree, and found
Torn with many wounds and bleeding,
Abu Midjan meek and bound.

And the Emir loosed him, saying,
As he gave his hand for sign,
"Never more shall Saad's fetters
Chafe thee for a draught of wine."

Three times to the ground in silence
Abu Midjan bent his head;
Then with glowing eyes uplifted,
To the Emir spake and said:

"While an earthly lord controlled me,
All things for the wine I bore;
Now, since God alone shall judge me,
Abu Midjan drinks no more."

The Weaver

All day, all day, round the clacking net
The weaver's fingers fly:
Gray dreams like frozen mists are set
In the hush of the weaver's eye;
A voice from the dusk is calling yet,
"Oh, come away, or we die!"

Without is a horror of hosts that fight,
That rest not, and cease not to kill,
The thunder of feet and the cry of flight,

A slaughter weird and shrill;
Gray dreams are set in the weaver's sight,
The weaver is weaving still.

"Come away, dear soul, come away, or we die;
Hear'st thou the moan and the rush! Come away;
The people are slain at the gates, and they fly;
The kind God hath left them this day;
The battle-axe cleaves, and the foemen cry,
And the red swords swing and slay."

"Nay, wife, what boots it to fly from pain,
When pain is wherever we fly?
And death is a sweeter thing than a chain:
'Tis sweeter to sleep than to cry.
The kind God giveth the days that wane;
If the kind God hath said it, I die."

And the weaver wove, and the good wife fled,
And the city was made a tomb,
And a flame that shook from the rocks overhead
Shone into that silent room,
And touched like a wide red kiss on the dead
Brown weaver slain by his loom.

Yet I think that in some dim shadowy land,
Where no suns rise or set,
Where the ghost of a whilom loom doth stand
Round the dusk of its silken net,
Forever flyeth his shadowy hand,
And the weaver is weaving yet.

The Three Pilgrims

In days, when the fruit of men's labour was sparing,
And hearts were weary and nigh to break,
A sweet grave man with a beautiful bearing
Came to us once in the fields and spake.

He told us of Roma, the marvellous city,
And of One that came from the living God,
The Virgins' Son, who in heavenly pity,
Bore for His people the rood and rod,

And how at Roma the gods were broken,
The new was strong, and the old nigh dead,
And love was more than a bare word spoken,
For the sick were healed and the poor were fed;

And we sat mute at his feet, and hearkened:
The grave man came in an hour; and went,
But a new light shone on a land long darkened;

The toil was weary, the fruit was spent:

So we came south, till we saw the city,
Speeding three of us, hand in hand,
Seeking peace and the bread of pity,
Journeying out of the Umbrian land;

Till we saw from the hills in a dazzled coma
Over the vines that the wind made shiver,
Tower on tower, the great city Roma,
Palace and temple, and winding river:

And we stood long in a dream and waited,
Watching and praying and purified,
And came at last to the walls belated,
Entering in at the eventide:

And many met us with song and dancing,
Mantled in skins and crowned with flowers,
Waving goblets and torches glancing;
Faces drunken, that grinned in ours:

And one, that ran in the midst, came near us
"Crown yourselves for the feast," he said,
But we cried out, that the God might hear us,
"Where is Jesus, the living bread?"

And they took us each by the hand with laughter;
Their eyes were haggard and red with wine:
They haled us on, and we followed after,
"We will show you the new God's shrine."

Ah, woe to our tongues, that, forever unsleeping,
Harp and uncover the old hot care,
The soothing ash from the embers sweeping,
Wherever the soles of our sad feet fare.

Ah, we were simple of mind, not knowing,
How dreadful the heart of a man might be;
But the knowledge of evil is mighty of growing;
Only the deaf and the blind are free.

We came to a garden of beauty and pleasure
It was not the way that our own feet chose
Where a revel was whirling in many a measure,
And the myriad roar of a great crowd rose;

And the midmost round of the garden was reddened
With pillars of fire in a great high ring
One look and our souls forever were deadened,
Though our feet yet move, and our dreams yet sting;

For we saw that each was a live man flaming,
Limbs that a human mother bore,
And a thing of horror was done, past naming,
And the crowd spun round, and we saw no more.

And he that ran in the midst, descrying,
Lifted his hand with a foul red sneer,
And smote us each and the other, crying,
"Thus we worship the new God here.

"The Cæsar comes, and the people's pæans
Hail his name for the new made light,
Pitch and the flesh of the Galileans,
Torches fit for a Roman night;"

And we fell down to the earth, and sickened,
Moaning, three of us, head by head,
"Where is He, whom the good God quickened?
Where is Jesus, the living bread?"

Yet ever we heard, in the foul mirth turning,
Man and woman and child go by,
And ever the yells of the charred men burning,
Piercing heavenward, cry on cry;

And we lay there, till the frightful revel
Died in the dawn with a few short moans
Of some that knelt in the wan and level
Shadows, that fell from the blackened bones.

Numb with horror and sick with pity,
The heart of each as an iron weight,
We crept in the dawn from the awful city,
Journeying out of the seaward gate.

The great sun came from the sea before us;
A soft wind blew from the scented south;
But our eyes knew not of the steps that bore us
Down to the ships at the Tiber's mouth;

And we prayed then, as we turned our faces
Over the sea to the living God,
That our ways might be in the fierce bare places,
Where never the foot of a live man trod:

And we set sail in the noon not caring.
Whither the prow of the dark ship came,
No more over the old ways faring;
For the sea was cold, but the land was flame:

And the keen ship sped, and a deadly coma
Blotted away from our eyes forever,

Tower on tower, the great city Roma,
Palace and temple and yellow river.

The Coming Of Winter

Out of the Northland sombre weirds are calling;
A shadow falleth southward day by day;
Sad summer's arms grow cold; his fire is falling;
His feet draw back to give the stern one way.

It is the voice and shadow of the slayer,
Slayer of loves, sweet world, slayer of dreams;
Make sad thy voice with sober plaint and prayer;
Make gray thy woods, and darken all thy streams.

Black grows the river, blacker drifts the eddy:
The sky is grey; the woods are cold below:
Oh make thy bosom, and thy sad lips ready,
For the cold kisses of the folding snow.

Easter Eve

Hear me, Brother, gently met;
Just a little, turn not yet,
Thou shalt laugh, and soon forget:
Now the midnight draweth near.
I have little more to tell;
Soon with hollow stroke and knell,
Thou shalt count the palace bell,
Calling that the hour is here.

Burdens black and strange to bear,
I must tell, and thou must share,
Listening with that stony stare,
Even as many a man before.
Years have lightly come and gone
In their jocund unison.
But the tides of life roll on
They remember now no more.

Once upon a night of glee,
In an hour of revelry,
As I wandered restlessly,
I beheld with burning eye,
How a pale procession rolled
Through a quarter quaint and old,
With its banners and its gold,
And the crucifix went by.

Well I knew that body brave
That was pierced and hung to save,
But my flesh was now a grave

For the soul that gnashed within.
He that they were bearing by,
With their banners white and high,
He was pure, and foul was I,
And his whiteness mocked my sin.

Ah, meseemed that even he,
Would not wait to look on me,
In my years and misery,
Things that he alone could heal.
In mine eyes I felt the flame
Of a rage that nought could tame,
And I cried and cursed his name,
Till my brain began to reel.

In a moment I was 'ware,
How that many watching there,
Fearfully with blanch and stare,
Crossed themselves, and shrank away;
Then upon my reeling mind,
Like a sharp blow from behind,
Fell the truth, and left me blind,
Hopeless now, and all astray.

O'er the city wandering wide,
Seeking but some place to hide,
Where the sounds of mirth had died,
Through the shaken night I stole;
From the ever-eddying stream
Of the crowds that did but seem
Like processions in a dream
To my empty echoing soul.

Till I came at last alone
To a hidden street of stone,
Where the city's monotone
On the silence fell no more.
Then I saw how one in white
With a footstep mute and light,
Through the shadow of the night
Like a spirit paced before.

And a sudden stillness came
Through my spirit and my frame,
And a spell without a name
Held me in his mystic track.
Though his presence seemed so mild,
Yet he led me like a child,
With a yearning strange and wild,
That I dared not turn me back.

Oh, I could not see his face,

Nor behold his utmost grace,
Yet I might not change my pace
Fastened by a strange belief;
For his steps were sad and slow,
And his hands hung straight below,
And his head was bowed, as though
Pressed by some immortal grief.

So I followed, yet not I
Held alone that company:
Every silent passer-by
Paled and turned and joined with me;
So we followed still and fleet,
While the city street by street,
Fell behind our rustling feet
Like a deadened memory.

Where the sound of sin and riot
Broke upon the night's dim quiet,
And the solemn bells hung nigh it
Echoed from their looming towers;
Where the mourners wept alway,
Watching for the morning grey;
Where the weary toiler lay,
Husbanding the niggard hours;

By the gates where all night long
Guests in many a joyous throng,
With the sound of dance and song,
Dreamed in golden palaces;
Still he passed, and door by door
Opened with a pale outpour,
And the revel rose no more
Hushed in deeper phantasies.

As we passed, the talk and stir
Of the quiet wayfarer
And the noisy banqueter
Died upon the midnight dim.
They that reeled in drunken glee
Shrank upon the trembling knee,
And their jests died pallidly,
As they rose and followed him.

From the street and from the hall,
From the flare of festival
None that saw him stayed, but all
Followed where his wonder would:
And our feet at first so few
Gathered as those white feet drew,
Till at last our number grew
To a pallid multitude;

And the hushed and awful beat
Of our pale unnumbered feet
Made a murmur strange and sweet,
As we followed evermore.
Now the night was almost passed,
And the dawn was overcast,
When the stranger stayed at last
At a great cathedral door.

Never word the stranger said,
But he slowly raised his head,
And the vast doors openèd
By an unseen hand withdrawn;
And in silence wave on wave,
Like an army from the grave,
Up the aisles and up the nave,
All that spectral crowd rolled on.

As I followed close behind,
Knowledge like an awful wind
Seemed to blow my naked mind
Into darkness black and bare;
Yet with longing wild and dim,
And a terror vast and grim,
Nearer still I pressed to him,
Till I almost touched his hair.

From the gloom so strange and eery,
From the organ low and dreary,
Rose the wailing miserere,
By mysterious voices sung;
And a dim light shone, none knew,
How it came, or whence it grew,
From the dusky roof and through
All the solemn spaces flung.

But the stranger still passed on,
Till he reached the altar stone,
And with body white and prone
Sunk his forehead to the floor;
And I saw in my despair,
Standing like a spirit there,
How his head was bruised and bare,
And his hands were clenched before,

How his hair was fouled and knit
With the blood that clotted it,
Where the prickled thorns had bit
In his crownèd agony;
In his hands so wan and blue,
Leaning out, I saw the two

Marks of where the nails pierced through,
Once on gloomy Calvary.

Then with trembling throat I owned
All my dark sin unatoned,
Telling it with lips that moaned,
And methought an echo came
From the bended crowd below,
Each one breathing faint and low,
Sins that none but he might know:
"Master I did curse thy name."

And I saw him slowly rise
With his sad unearthly eyes,
Meeting mine with meek surprise,
And a voice came solemnly.
"Never more on mortal ground
For thy soul shall rest be found,
But when bells at midnight sound
Thou must rise and come with me."

Then my forehead smote the floor,
Swooning, and I knew no more,
Till I heard the chancel door
Open for the choristers:
But the stranger's form was gone,
And the church was dim and lone:
Through the silence, one by one
Stole the early worshippers.

I am ageing now I know;
That was many years ago,
Yet or I shall rest below
In the grave where none intrude,
Night by night I roam the street,
And that awful form I meet,
And I follow pale and fleet,
With a ghostly multitude.

Every night I see his face,
With its sad and burdened grace,
And the torn and bloody trace,
That in hands and feet he has.
Once my life was dark and bad;
Now its days are strange and sad,
And the people call me mad:
See, they whisper as they pass.

Even now the echoes roll
From the swinging bells that toll;
It is midnight, now my soul
Hasten; for he glideth by.

Stranger, 'tis no phantasie:
Look! my master waits for me
Mutely, but thou canst not see
With thy mortal blinded eye.

The Organist

In his dim chapel day by day
The organist was wont to play,
And please himself with fluted reveries;
And all the spirit's joy and strife,
The longing of a tender life,
Took sound and form upon the ivory keys;
And though he seldom spoke a word,
The simple hearts that loved him heard
His glowing soul in these.

One day as he was wrapped, a sound
Of feet stole near; he turned and found
A little maid that stood beside him there.
She started, and in shrinking-wise
Besought him with her liquid eyes
And little features, very sweet and spare.
"You love the music, child," he said,
And laid his hand upon her head,
And smoothed her matted hair.

She answered, "At the door one day
I sat and heard the organ play;
I did not dare to come inside for fear;
But yesterday, a little while,
I crept half up the empty aisle
And heard the music sounding sweet and clear;
To-day I thought you would not mind,
For, master dear, your face was kind,
And so I came up here."

"You love the music then," he said,
And still he stroked her golden head,
And followed out some winding reverie;
"And you are poor?" said he at last;
The maiden nodded, and he passed
His hand across his forehead dreamingly;
"And will you be my friend?" he spake,
"And on the organ learn to make
Grand music here with me?"

And all the little maiden's face
Was kindled with a grateful grace;
"Oh, master, teach me; I will slave for thee!"
She cried; and so the child grew dear
To him, and slowly year by year

He taught her all the organ's majesty;
And gave her from his slender store
Bread and warm clothing, that no more
Her cheeks were pinched to see.

And year by year the maiden grew
Taller and lovelier, and the hue
Deepened upon her tender cheeks untried.
Rounder, and queenlier, and more fair
Her form grew, and her golden hair
Fell yearly richer at the master's side.
In speech and bearing, form and face,
Sweeter and graver, grace by grace,
Her beauties multiplied.

And sometimes at his work a glow
Would touch him, and he murmured low,
"How beautiful she is?" and bent his head;
And sometimes when the day went by
And brought no maiden he would sigh,
And lean and listen for her velvet tread;
And he would drop his hands and say,
"My music cometh not to-day;
Pray God she be not dead!"

So the sweet maiden filled his heart,
And with her growing grew his art,
For day by day more wondrously he played.
Such heavenly things the master wrought,
That in his happy dreams he thought
The organ's self did love the gold-haired maid:
But she, the maiden, never guessed
What prayers for her in hours of rest
The sombre organ prayed.

At last, one summer morning fair,
The maiden came with braided hair
And took his hands, and held them eagerly.
"To-morrow is my wedding day;
Dear master, bless me that the way
Of life be smooth, not bitter unto me."
He stirred not; but the light did go
Out of his shrunken cheeks, and oh!
His head hung heavily.

"You love him, then?" "I love him well,"
She answered, and a numbness fell
Upon his eyes and all his heart that bled.
A glory, half a smile, abode
Within the maiden's eyes and glowed
Upon her parted lips. The master said,
"God bless and bless thee, little maid,

With peace and long delight," and laid
His hands upon her head.

And she was gone; and all that day
The hours crept up and slipped away,
And he sat still, as moveless as a stone.
The night came down, with quiet stars,
And darkened him: in colored bars
Along the shadowy aisle the moonlight shone.
And then the master woke and passed
His hands across the keys at last,
And made the organ moan.

The organ shook, the music wept;
For sometimes like a wail it crept
In broken moanings down the shadows drear;
And otherwhiles the sound did swell,
And like a sudden tempest fell
Through all the windows wonderful and clear.
The people gathered from the street,
And filled the chapel seat by seat
They could not choose but hear.

And there they sat till dawning light,
Nor ever stirred for awe. "To-night,
The master hath a noble mood," they said.
But on a sudden ceased the sound:
Like ghosts the people gathered round,
And on the keys they found his fallen head.
The silent organ had received
The master's broken heart relieved,
And he was white and dead.

The Monk

I

In Nino's chamber not a sound intrudes
Upon the midnight's tingling silentness,
Where Nino sits before his book and broods,
Thin and brow-burdened with some fine distress,
Some gloom that hangs about his mournful moods
His weary bearing and neglected dress:
So sad he sits, nor ever turns a leaf
Sorrow's pale miser o'er his hoard of grief.

II

Young Nino and Leonora, they had met
Once at a revel by some lover's chance,
And they were young with hearts already set
To tender thoughts, attunèd to romance;
Wherefore it seemed they never could forget
That winning touch, that one bewildering glance:

But found at last a shelter safe and sweet,
Where trembling hearts and longing hands might meet.

III

Ah, sweet their dreams, and sweet the life they led
With that great love that was their bosoms' all,
Yet ever shadowed by some circling dread
It gloomed at moments deep and tragical,
And so for many a month they seemed to tread
With fluttering hearts, whatever might befall,
Half glad, half sad, their sweet and secret way
To the soft tune of some old lover's lay.

IV

But she is gone, alas he knows not where,
Or how his life that tender gift should lose:
Indeed his love was ever full of care,
The hasty joys and griefs of him who woos,
Where sweet success is neighbour to despair,
With stolen looks and dangerous interviews:
But one long week she came not, nor the next,
And so he wandered here and there perplext;

V

Nor evermore she came. Full many days
He sought her at their trysts, devised deep schemes
To lure her back, and fell on subtle ways
To win some word of her; but all his dreams
Vanished like smoke, and then in sore amaze
From town to town, as one that crazèd seems,
He wandered, following in unhappy quest
Uncertain clues that ended like the rest.

VI

And now this midnight, as he sits forlorn,
The printed page for him no meaning bears;
With every word some torturing dream is born;
And every thought is like a step that scares
Old memories up to make him weep and mourn.
He cannot turn but from their latchless lairs,
The weary shadows of his lost delight
Rise up like dusk birds through the lonely night.

VII

And still with questions vain he probes his grief,
Till thought is wearied out, and dreams grow dim.
What bitter chance, what woe beyond belief
Could keep his lady's heart so hid from him?
Or was her love indeed but light and brief,
A passing thought, a moment's dreamy whim?
Aye there it stings, the woe that never sleeps:
Poor Nino leans upon his book, and weeps.

VIII

Until at length the sudden grief that shook
His piercèd bosom like a gust is past,
And laid full weary on the wide-spread book,
His eyes grow dim with slumber light and fast;
But scarcely have his dreams had time to look
On lands of kindlier promise, when aghast
He starts up softly, and in wondering wise
Listens atremble with wide open eyes.

IX

What sound was that? Who knocks like one in dread
With such swift hands upon his outer door?
Perhaps some beggar driven from his bed
By gnawing hunger he can bear no more,
Or questing traveller with confusèd tread,
Straying, bewildered in the midnight hoar.
Nino uprises, scared, he knows not how,
The dreams still pale about his burdened brow.

X

The heavy bolt he draws, and unawares
A stranger enters with slow steps, unsought,
A long robed monk, and in his hand he bears
A jewelled goblet curiously wrought;
But of his face beneath the cowl he wears
For all his searching Nino seeth nought;
And slowly past him with long stride he hies,
While Nino follows with bewildered eyes.

XI

Straight on he goes with dusky rustling gown.
His steps are soft, his hands are white and fine;
And still he bears the goblet on whose crown
A hundred jewels in the lamplight shine;
And ever from its edges dripping down
Falls with dark stain the rich and lustrous wine,
Wherefrom through all the chamber's shadowy deeps
A deadly perfume like a vapour creeps.

XII

And now he sets it down with careful hands
On the slim table's polished ebony;
And for a space as if in dreams he stands,
Close hidden in his sombre drapery.
"Oh lover, by thy lady's last commands,
I bid thee hearken, for I bear with me
A gift to give thee and a tale to tell
From her who loved thee, while she lived, too well."

XIII

The stranger's voice falls slow and solemnly.
Tis soft, and rich, and wondrous deep of tone;
And Nino's face grows white as ivory,
Listening fast-rooted like a shape of stone.
Ah, blessed saints, can such a dark thing be?
And was it death, and is Leonora gone?
Oh, love is harsh, and life is frail indeed,
That gives men joy, and then so makes them bleed.

XIV
"There is the gift I bring"; the stranger's head
Turns to the cup that glitters at his side:
"And now my tongue draws back for very dread,
Unhappy youth, from what it must not hide.
The saddest tale that ever lips have said;
Yet thou must know how sweet Leonora died,
A broken martyr for love's weary sake,
And left this gift for thee to leave or take."

XV
Poor Nino listens with that marble face,
And eyes that move not, strangely wide and set.
The monk continues with his mournful grace:
"She told me, Nino, how you often met
In secret, and your plighted loves kept pace
Together, tangled in the self-same net;
Your dream's dark danger and its dread you knew,
And still you met, and still your passion grew.

XVI
"And aye with that luxurious fire you fed
Your dangerous longing daily, crumb by crumb;
Nor ever cared that still above your head
The shadow grew; for that your lips were dumb.
You knew full keenly you could never wed:
'Twas all a dream: the end must surely come;
For not on thee her father's eyes were turned
To find a son, when mighty lords were spurned.

XVII
"Thou knowest that new-sprung prince, that proud up-start,
Pisa's new tyrant with his armèd thralls,
Who bends of late to take the people's part,
Yet plays the king among his marble halls,
Whose gloomy palace in our city's heart
Frowns like a fortress with its loop-holed walls.
'Twas him he sought for fair Leonora's hand,
That so his own declining house might stand.

XVIII
"The end came soon; 'twas never known to thee;
But, when your love was scarce a six months old,

She sat one day beside her father's knee,
And in her ears the dreadful thing was told.
Within one month her bridal hour should be
With Messer Gianni for his power and gold;
And as she sat with whitened lips the while,
The old man kissed her, with his crafty smile.

XIX
"Poor pallid lady, all the woe she felt
Thou, wretched Nino, thou alone canst know.
Down at his feet with many a moan she knelt,
And prayed that he would never wound her so.
Ah, tender saints! it was a sight to melt
The flintiest heart; but his could never glow.
He sat with clenchèd hands and straightened head,
And frowned, and glared, and turned from white to red.

XX
"And still with cries about his knees she clung,
Her tender bosom broken with her care.
His words were brief, with bitter fury flung:
'The father's will the child must meekly bear;
I am thy father, thou a girl and young.'
Then to her feet she rose in her despair,
And cried with tightened lips and eyes aglow,
One daring word, a straight and simple, "No"!

XXI
"Her father left her with wild words, and sent
Rough men, who dragged her to a dungeon deep,
Where many a weary soul in darkness pent
For many a year had watched the slow days creep,
And there he left her for his dark intent,
Where madness breeds and sorrows never sleep.
Coarse robes he gave her, and her lips he fed
With bitter water and a crust of bread.

XXII
"And day by day still following out his plan,
He came to her, and with determined spite
Strove with soft words and then with curse and ban
To bend her heart so wearied to his might,
And aye she bode his bitter pleasure's span,
As one that hears, but hath not sense or sight.
Ah, Nino, still her breaking heart held true:
Poor lady sad, she had no thought but you.

XXIII
"The father tired at last and came no more,
But in his settled anger bade prepare
The marriage feast with all luxurious store,
With pomps, and shows and splendors rich and rare;

And so in toil another fortnight wore,
Nor knew she aught what things were in the air,
Till came the old lord's message brief and coarse:
Within three days she should be wed by force.

XXIV
"And all that noon and weary night she lay,
Poor child, like death upon her prison stone,
And none that came to her but crept away,
Sickened at heart to see her lips so moan,
Her eyes so dim within their sockets grey,
Her tender cheeks so thin and ghastly grown;
But when the next morn's light began to stir,
She sent and prayed that I might be with her.

XXV
"This boon he gave: perchance he deemed that I,
The chaplain of his house, her childhood's friend,
With patient tones and holy words, might try
To soothe her purpose to his gainful end.
I bowed full low before his crafty eye,
But knew my heart had no base help to lend.
That night with many a silent prayer I came
To poor Leonora in her grief and shame.

XXVI
"But she was strange to me: I could not speak
For glad amazement, mixed with some dark fear;
I saw her stand no longer pale and weak,
But a proud maiden, queenly and most clear,
With flashing eyes and vermeil in her cheek:
And on the little table, set anear,
I marked two goblets of rare workmanship
With some strange liquor crownèd to the lip.

XXVII
"And then she ran to me and caught my hand,
Tightly imprisoned in her meagre twain,
And like the ghost of sorrow she did stand,
And eyed me softly with a liquid pain:
'Oh father, grant, I pray thee, I command,
One boon to me, I'll never ask again,
One boon to me and to my love, to both;
Dear father, grant, and bind it with an oath.'

XXVIII
"This granted I, and then with many a wail
She told me all the story of your woe,
And when she finished, lightly but most pale,
To those two brimming goblets she did go,
And one she took within her fingers frail,
And looked down smiling in its crimson glow:

'And now thine oath I'll tell; God grant to thee
No rest in grave, if thou be false to me.

XXIX

"'Alas, poor me! whom cruel hearts would wed
On the sad morrow to that wicked lord;
But I'll not go; nay, rather I'll be dead,
Safe from their frown and from their bitter word.
Without my Nino life indeed were sped;
And sith we two can never more accord
In this drear world, so weary and perplext,
We'll die, and win sweet pleasure in the next.

XXX

"'Oh father, God will never give thee rest,
If thou be false to what thy lips have sworn,
And false to love, and false to me distressed,
A helpless maid, so broken and outworn.
This cup, she put it softly to her breast
I pray thee carry, ere the morrow morn,
To Nino's hand, and tell him all my pain;
This other with mine own lips I will drain.'

XXXI

"Slowly she raised it to her lips, the while
I darted forward, madly fain to seize
Her dreadful hands, but with a sudden wile
She twisted and sprang from me with bent knees,
And rising turned upon me with a smile,
And drained her goblet to the very lees.
'Oh priest, remember, keep thine oath,' she cried,
And the spent goblet fell against her side.

XXXII

"And then she moaned and murmured like a bell:
'My Nino, my sweet Nino!' and no more
She said, but fluttered like a bird and fell
Lifeless as marble to the footworn floor;
And there she lies even now in lonely cell,
Poor lady, pale with all the grief she bore,
She could not live, and still be true to thee,
And so she's gone where no rude hands can be."

XXXIII

The monk's voice pauses like some mournful flute,
Whose pondered closes for sheer sorrow fail,
And then with hand that seems as it would suit
A soft girl best, it is so light and frail,
He turns half round, and for a moment mute
Points to the goblet, and so ends his tale:
"Mine oath is kept, thy lady's last command;
'Tis but a short hour since it left her hand."

XXXIV

So ends the stranger: surely no man's tongue
Was e'er so soft, or half so sweet, as his.
Oft as he listened, Nino's heart had sprung
With sudden start as from a spectre's kiss;
For deep in many a word he deemed had rung
The liquid fall of some loved emphasis;
And so it pierced his sorrow to the core,
The ghost of tones that he should hear no more.

XXXV

But now the tale is ended, and still keeps
The stranger hidden in his dusky weed;
And Nino stands, wide-eyed, as one that sleeps,
And dimly wonders how his heart doth bleed.
Anon he bends, yet neither moans nor weeps,
But hangs atremble, like a broken reed;
"Ah! bitter fate, that lured and sold us so,
Poor lady mine; alas for all our woe!"

XXXVI

But even as he moans in such dark mood,
His wandering eyes upon the goblet fall.
Oh, dreaming heart! Oh, strange ingratitude!
So to forget his lady's lingering call,
Her parting gift, so rich, so crimson-hued,
The lover's draught, that shall be cure for all.
He lifts the goblet lightly from its place,
And smiles, and rears it with his courtly grace.

XXXVII

"Oh, lady sweet, I shall not long delay:
This gift of thine shall bring me to thine eyes.
Sure God will send on no unpardoned way
The faithful soul, that at such bidding dies.
When thou art gone, I cannot longer stay
To brave this world with all its wrath and lies,
Where hands of stone and tongues of dragon's breath
Have bruised mine angel to her piteous death."

XXXVIII

And now the gleaming goblet hath scarce dyed
His lips' thin pallor with its deathly red,
When Nino starts in wonder, fearful-eyed,
For, lo! the stranger with outstretchèd head
Springs at his face one soft and sudden stride,
And from his hand the deadly cup hath sped,
Dashed to the ground, and all it's seeded store
Runs out like blood upon the marble floor.

XXXIX

"Oh Nino, my sweet Nino! speak to me,
Nor stand so strange, nor look so deathly pale.
'Twas all to prove thy heart's deaf constancy
I brought that cup and told that piteous tale.
Ah! chains and cells and cruel treachery
Are weak indeed when women's hearts assail.
Art angry, Nino?" 'Tis no monk that cries,
But sweet Leonora with her love-lit eyes.

XL
She dashes from her brow the pented hood;
The dusky robe falls rustling to her feet;
And there she stands, as aye in dreams she stood.
Ah, Nino, see! Sure man did never meet
So warm a flower from such a sombre bud,
So trembling fair, so wan, so pallid sweet.
Aye, Nino, down like saint upon thy knee,
And soothe her hands with kisses warm and free.

XLI
And now with broken laughter on her lips,
And now with moans remembering of her care,
She weeps, and smiles, and like a child she slips
Her lily fingers through his curly hair,
The while her head with all it's sweet she dips,
Close to his ear, to soothe and murmur there;
"Oh, Nino, I was hid so long from thee,
That much I doubted what thy love might be.

XLII
"And though 'twas cruel hard of me to try
Thy faithful heart with such a fearful test,
Yet now thou canst be happy, sweet, as I
Am wondrous happy in thy truth confessed.
To haggard death indeed thou needst not fly
To find the softness of thy lady's breast;
For such a gift was never death's to give,
But thou shalt have me for thy love, and live.

XLIII
"Dost see these cheeks, my Nino? they're so thin,
Not round and soft, as when thou touched them last:
So long with bitter rage they pent me in,
Like some poor thief in lonely dungeon cast;
Only this night through every bolt and gin
By cunning stealth I wrought my way at last.
Straight to thine heart I fled, unfaltering,
Like homeward pigeon with uncagèd wing.

XLIV
"Nay, Nino, kneel not; let me hear thee speak.
We must not tarry long; the dawn is nigh."

So rises he, for very gladness weak;
But half in fear that yet the dream may fly,
He touches mutely mouth and brow and cheek;
Till in his ear she 'gins to plead and sigh:
"Dear love, forgive me for that cruel tale,
That stung thine heart and made thy lips so pale."

XLV
And so he folds her softly with quick sighs,
And both with murmurs warm and musical
Talk and retalk, with dim or smiling eyes,
Of old delights and sweeter days to fall:
And yet not long, for, ere the starlit skies
Grow pale above the city's eastern wall,
They rise, with lips and happy hands withdrawn,
And pass out softly into the dawn.

XLVI
For Nino knows the captain of a ship,
The friend of many journeys, who may be
This very morn will let his cables slip
For the warm coast of sunny Sicily.
There in Palermo, at the harbour's lip,
A brother lives, of tried fidelity:
So to the quays by hidden ways they wend
In the pale morn, nor do they miss their friend.

XLVII
And ere the shadow of another night
Hath darkened Pisa, many a foe shall stray
Through Nino's home, with eyes malignly bright
In wolfish quest, but shall not find his prey:
The while those lovers in their white-winged flight
Shall see far out upon the twilight grey,
Behind, the glimmer of the sea, before,
The dusky outlines of a kindlier shore.

The Child's Music Lesson
Why weep ye in your innocent toil at all?
Sweet little hands, why halt and tremble so?
Full many a wrong note falls, but let it fall!
Each note to me is like a golden glow;
Each broken cadence like a morning call;
Nay, clear and smooth I would not have you go,
Soft little hands, upon the curtained threshold set
Of this long life of labour, and unrestful fret.

Soft sunlight flickers on the checkered green:
Warm winds are stirring round my dreaming seat:
Among the yellow pumpkin blooms, that lean
Their crumpled rims beneath the heavy heat,

The stripèd bees in lazy labour glean
From bell to bell with golden-feathered feet;
Yet even here the voices of hard life go by;
Outside, the city strains with its eternal cry.

Here, as I sit, the sunlight on my face,
And shadows of green leaves upon mine eyes
My heart, a garden in a hidden place,
Is full of folded buds of memories.
Stray hither then with all your old time grace,
Child-voices, trembling from the uncertain keys;
Play on, ye little fingers, touch the settled gloom,
And quickly, one by one, my waiting buds will bloom.

Ah me, I may not set my feet again
In any part of that old garden dear,
Or pluck one widening blossom, for my pain;
But only at the wicket gaze I here:
Old scents creep into mine inactive brain,
Smooth scents of things, I may not come anear;
I see, far off, old beaten pathways they adorn;
I cannot feel with hands the blossom or the thorn.

Toil on, sweet hands; once more I see the child;
The little child, that was myself, appears,
And all the old-time beauties, undefined,
Shine back to me across the opening years,
Quick griefs, that made the tender bosom wild,
Short blinding gusts, that died in passionate tears,
Sweet life, with all its change, that now so happy seems,
With all its child-heart glories, and untutored dreams.

Play on into the golden sunshine so,
Sweeter than all great artists' labouring:
I too was like you once, an age ago:
God keep you, dimpled fingers, for you bring
Quiet gliding ghosts to me of joy and woe,
No certain things at all that thrill or sting,
But only sounds and scents and savours of things bright,
No joy or aching pain; but only dim delight.

An Athenian Reverie
How the returning days, one after one,
Come ever in their rhythmic round, unchanged,
Yet from each loopèd robe for every man
Some new thing falls. Happy is he
Who fronts them without fear, and like the gods
Looks out unanxiously on each day's gift
With calmly curious eye. How many things
Even in a little space, both good and ill,
Have fallen on me, and yet in all of them

The keen experience or the smooth remembrance
Hath found some sweet. It scarcely seems a month
Since we saw Crete; so swiftly sped the days,
Borne onward with how many changing scenes,
Filled with how many crowding memories.
Not soon shall I forget them, the stout ship,
All the tense labour with the windy sea,
The cloud-wrapped heights of Crete, beheld far off,
And white Cytæon with its stormy pier,
The fruitful valleys, the wild mountain road,
And those long days of ever-vigilant toil,
Scarcely with sleepless craft and unmoved front
Escaping robbers, that quiet restful eve
At rich Gortyna, where we lay and watched
The dripping foliage, and the darkening fields,
And over all huge-browed above the night
Ida's great summit with it's fiery crown;
And then once more the stormy treacherous sea,
The noisy ship, the seamen's vehement cries,
That battled with the whistling wind, the feet
Reeling upon the swaying deck, and eyes
Strained anxiously toward land; ah, with what joy
At last the busy pier at Nauplia,
Rest and firm shelter for our racking brains:
Most sweet of all, most dear to memory
That journey with Euktemon through the hills
By fair Cleonæ and the lofty pass;
Then Corinth with its riotous jollity,
Remembered like a reeling dream; and here
Good Theron's wedding, and this festal day;
And I, chief helper in its various rites,
Not least, commissioned through these wakeful hours
To dream before the quiet thalamos,
Unsleeping, like some full-grown bearded Eros,
The guardian of love's sweetest mysteries.
To-morrow I shall hear again the din
Of the loosed cables, and the rowers' chaunt,
The rattled cordage and the plunging oars.
Once more the bending sail shall bear us on
Across the level of the laughing sea.
Ere mid-day we shall see far off behind us,
Faint as the summit of a sultry cloud,
The white Acropolis. Past Sunium
With rushing keel, the long Euboean strand,
Hymettus and the pine-dark hills shall fade
Into the dusk: at Andros we shall water,
And ere another starlight hush the shores
From seaward valleys catch upon the wind
The fragrance of old Chian vintages.
At Chios many things shall fall, but none
Can trace the future; rather let me dream
Of what is now, and what hath been, for both

Are fraught with life.

Here the unbroken silence
Awakens thought and makes remembrance sweet.
How solidly the brilliant moonlight shines
Into the courts; beneath the colonnades
How dense the shadows. I can scarcely see
Yon painted Dian on the darkened wall;
Yet how the gloom hath made her real. What sound,
Piercing the leafy covert of her couch,
Hath startled her. Perchance some prowling wolf,
Or luckless footsteps of the stealthy Pan,
Creeping at night among the noiseless steeps
And hollows of the Erymanthian woods,
Roused her from sleep. With listening head,
Snatched bow, and quiver lightly slung, she stands,
And peers across that dim and motionless glade,
Beckoning about her heels the wakeful dogs;
Yet Dian, thus alert, is but a dream,
Making more real this brooding quietness.
How strong and wonderful is night! Mankind
Has yielded all to one sweet helplessness:
Thought, labour, strife and all activities
Have ebbed like fever. The smooth tide of sleep,
Rolling across the fields of Attica,
Hath covered all the labouring villages.
Even great Athens with her busy hands
And busier tongues lies quiet beneath it's waves.
Only a steady murmur seems to come
Up from her silentness, as if the land
Were breathing heavily in dreams. Abroad
No creature stirs, not even the reveller,
Staggering, unlanterned, from the cool Piræus,
With drunken shout. The remnants of the feast,
The crumpled cushions and the broken wreathes,
Lie scattered in yon shadowy court, whose stones
Through the warm hours drink up the staining wine.
The bridal oxen in their well-filled stalls
Sleep, mindless of the happy weight they drew.
The torch is charred; the garlands at the door,
So gay at morning with their bright festoons,
Hang limp and withered; and the joyous flutes
Are empty of all sound. Only my brain
Holds now in it's remote unsleeping depths
The echo of the tender hymenæos
And memory of the modest lips that sang it.
Within the silent thalamos the queen,
The sea-sprung radiant Cytherean reigns,
And with her smiling lips and fathomless eyes
Regards the lovers, knowing that this hour
Is theirs once only. Earth and thought and time
Lie far beyond them, a great gulf of joy,

Absorbing fear, regret and every grief,
A warm eternity: or now perchance
Night and the very weight of happiness,
Unsought, have turned upon their tremulous eyes
The mindless stream of sleep; nor do they care
If dawn should never come.

How joyously
These hours have gone with all their pictured scenes,
A string of golden beads for memory
To finger over in her moods, or stay
The hunger of some wakeful hour like this,
The flowers, the myrtles, the gay bridal train,
The flutes and pensive voices, the white robes,
The shower of sweet-meats, and the jovial feast,
The bride cakes, and the teeming merriment,
Most beautiful of all, most sweet to name,
The good Lysippe with her down-cast eyes,
Touched with soft fear, half scared at all the noise,
Whose tears were ready as her laughter, fresh,
And modest as some pink anemone.
How young she looked, and how her smiling lips
Betrayed her happiness. Ah, who can tell,
How often, when no watchful eye was near,
Her eager fingers, trembling and ashamed,
Essayed the apple-pips, or strewed the floor
With broken poppy petals. Next to her,
Theron himself the gladest goodliest figure,
His honest face ruddy with health and joy,
And smiling like the Ægean, when the sun
Hangs high in heaven, and the freshening wind
Comes in from Melos, rippling all its floor:
And there was Manto too, the good old crone,
So dear to children with her store of tales,
Warmed with new life: how to her old grey face
And withered limbs the very dance of youth
Seemed to return, and in her aged eyes
The waning fire rekindled: little Mæon,
That mischievous satyr with his tipsy wreath,
Who kept us laughing at his pranks, and made
Old Pyrrho angry. Him too sleep hath bound
Upon his rough-hewn couch with subtle thong,
Crowding his brain with odd fantastic shapes.
Even in sleep his little limbs, I think,
Twitch restlessly, and still his tongue gibes on
With inarticulate murmur. Ah, quaint Mæon!
And Manto, poor old Manto, what dim dreams
Of darkly-moving chaos and slow shapes
Of things that creep encumbered with huge burdens
Gloom and infest her through these dragging hours,
Haunting the wavering soul, so near the grave?
But all things journey to the same quiet end

At last, life, joy and every form of motion.
Nothing stands still. Not least inevitable,
The sad recession of this passionate love,
Whose panting fires, so soon and with such grief,
Burn down to ash.

Ai! Ai! 'tis a strange madness
To give up thought, ambition, liberty,
And all the rooted custom of our days,
Even life itself for one all pampering dream,
That withers like those garlands at the door;
And yet I have seen many excellent men
Besotted thus, and some that bore till death,
In the crook'd vision and embittered tongue,
The effect of this strange poison, like a scar,
An ineradicable hurt; but Fate,
Who deals more wondrously in this disease
Even than in others, yet doth sometimes will
To make the same thing unto different men
Evil or good. Was not Demetrios happy,
Who wore his fetters with such grace, and spent
On Chione, the Naxian, that shrewd girl,
His fortune and his youth, yet, while she lived,
Enjoyed the rich reward? He seemed like one,
That trod on wind, and I remember well,
How when she died in that remorseless plague,
And I alone stood with him at the pyre,
He shook me with his helpless passionate grief.
And honest Agathon, the married man,
Whose boyish fondness for his pretty wife
We smiled at, and yet envied; at the close
Of each day's labour how he posted home,
And thence no bait, however plumed, could draw him.
We laughed, but envied him. How sweet she looked
That morning at the Dyonisia,
With her rare eyes and modest girlish grace,
Leading her two small children by the palm.
I too might marry, if the faithful gods
Would promise me such joy as Agathon's.
Perhaps some day but no, I am not one
To clip my wings, and wind about my feet
A net, whose self-made meshes are as stern
As they are soft. To me is ever present
The outer world with its untravelled paths,
The wanderer's dream, the itch to see new things.
A single tie could never bind me fast,
For life, this joyous, busy, ever-changing life,
Is only dear to me with liberty,
With space of earth for feet to travel in
And space of mind for thought.

Not so for all;

To most men life is but a common thing,
The hours a sort of coin to barter with,
Whose worth is reckoned by the sum they buy
In gold, or power, or pleasure; each short day
That brings not these deemed fruitless as dry sand.
Their lives are but a blind activity,
And death to them is but the end of motion,
Grey children who have madly eat and drunk,
Won the high seats or filled their chests with gold.
And yet for all their years have never seen
The picture of their lives, or how life looks
To him who hath the deep uneager eye,
How sweet and large and beautiful it was,
How strange the part they played. Like him who sits
Beneath some mighty tree, with half-closed eyes,
At ease rejoicing in its murmurous shade,
Yet never once awakes from his dull dream
To mark with curious joy the kingly trunk,
The sweeping boughs and tower of leaves that gave it,
Even so the most of men; they take the gift,
And care not for the giver. Strange indeed
Are they, and pitiable beyond measure,
Who, thus unmindful of their wretchedness,
Crowd at life's bountiful gates, like fattening beggars,
Greedy and blind. For see how rich a thing
Life is to him who sees, to whom each hour
Brings some fresh wonder to be brooded on,
Adds some new group or studied history
To that wrought sculpture, that our watchful dreams
Cast up upon the broad expanse of time,
As in a never-finished frieze, not less
The little things that most men pass unmarked
Than those that shake mankind. Happy is he,
Who, as a watcher, stands apart from life,
From all life and his own, and thus from all,
Each thought, each deed, and each hour's brief event,
Draws the full beauty, sucks its meaning dry.
For him this life shall be a tranquil joy.
He shall be quiet and free. To him shall come
No gnawing hunger for the coarser touch,
No mad ambition with its fateful grasp;
Sorrow itself shall sway him like a dream.

How full life is; how many memories
Flash, and shine out, when thought is sharply stirred;
How the mind works, when once the wheels are loosed,
How nimbly, with what swift activity.
I think, 'tis strange that men should ever sleep,
There are so many things to think upon,
So many deeds, so many thoughts to weigh,
To pierce, and plumb them to the silent depth.
Yet in that thought I do rebuke myself,

Too little given to probe the inner heart,
But rather wont, with the luxurious eye,
To catch from life it's outer loveliness,
Such things as do but store the joyous memory
With food for solace rather than for thought,
Like light-lined figures on a painted jar.
I wonder where Euktemon is to-night,
Euktemon with his rough and fitful talk,
His moody gesture and defiant stride;
How strange, how bleak and unapproachable;
And yet I liked him from the first. How soon
We know our friends, through all disguise of mood,
Discerning by a subtle touch of spirit
The honest heart within. Euktemon's glance
Betrayed him with it's gusty friendliness,
Flashing at moments from the clouded brow,
Like brave warm sunshine, and his laughter too,
So rare, so sudden, so contagious,
How at some merry scene, some well-told tale,
Or swift invention of the wingèd wit,
It broke like thunderous water, rolling out
In shaken peals on the delighted ear.
Yet no man would have dreamed, who saw us two
That first grey morning on the pier at Crete,
That friendship could have forged thus easily
A bond so subtle and so sure between us;
He, gloomy and austere; I, full of thought
As he, yet in an adverse mood, at ease,
Lifting with lighter hands the lids of life,
Untortured by its riddles; he, whose smiles
Were rare and sudden as the autumn sun;
I, to whom smiles are ever near the lip.
And yet I think he loved me too; my mood
Was not unpleasant to him, though I know
At times I teased him with my flickering talk.
How self-immured he was; for all our converse
I gathered little, little, of his life,
A bitter trial to me, who love to learn
The changes of men's outer circumstance,
The strokes that fate has shaped them with, and so,
Fitting to these their present speech and favour,
Discern the thought within. From him I gleaned
Nothing. At the least word, however guarded,
That sought to try the fastenings of his life
With prying hands, how mute and dark he grew,
And like the cautious tortoise at a touch
Drew in beneath his shell.

But ah, how sweet
The memory of that long untroubled day,
To me so joyous, and so free from care,
Spent as I love on foot, our first together,

When fate and the reluctant sea at last
Had given us safely to dry land; the tramp
From grey Mycenæ by the pass to Corinth,
The smooth white road, the soft caressing air,
Full of the scent of blossoms, the clear sky,
Strewn lightly with the little tardy clouds,
Old Helios' scattered flock, the low-branched oaks
And fountained resting-places, the cool nooks,
Where eyes less darkened with life's use than mine
Perchance had caught the Naiads in their dreams,
Or won white glimpses of their flying heels.
How light our feet were: with what rhythmic strides
We left the long blue gulf behind us, sown
Far out with snowy sails; and how our hearts
Rose with the growth of morning, till we reached
That moss-hung fountain on the hillside near
Cleonæ, where the dark anemones
Cover the ground, and make it red like fire.
Could ever grief, I wonder, or fixed care,
Or even the lingering twilight of old age,
Divest for me such memories of their sweet?
Even Euktemon's obdurate mood broke down.
The odorous stillness, the serene bright air,
The leafy shadows, the warm blossoming earth,
Drew near with their voluptuous eloquence,
And melted him. Ah, what a talk we had!
How eagerly our nimble tongues ran on,
With linkèd wit, in joyous sympathy.
Such hours, I think, are better than long years
Of brooding loneliness, mind touching mind
To leaping life, and thought sustaining thought,
Till even the darkest chambers of grey time,
His ancient seats, and bolted mysteries,
Open their hoary doors, and at a look
Lay all their treasures bare. How, when our thought
Wheeling on ever bolder wings at last
Grew as it seemed too large for utterance,
We both fell silent, striving to recall
And grasp such things as in our daring mood
We had but glimpsed and leaped at; yet how long
We studied thus with absent eyes, I know not;
Our thought died slowly out; the busy road,
The voices of the passers-by, the change
Of garb and feature, and the various tongues
Absorbed us. Ah, how clearly I recall them!
For in these silent wakeful hours the mind
Is strangely swift. With what sharp lines
The shapes of things that even years have buried
Shine out upon the rapid memory,
Moving and warm like life. I can see now
The form of that tall peddler, whose strange wares,
Outlandish dialect and impudent gait

Awoke Euktemon's laughter. In mine ear
Is echoing still the cracking string of gibes,
They flung at one another. I remember too
The grey-haired merchant with his bold black eyes
And brace of slaves, the old ship captain tanned
With sweeping sea-winds and the pitiless sun,
But best of all that dainty amorous pair,
Whose youthful spirit neither heat nor toil
Could conquer. What a charming group they made?
The creaking litter and the long brown poles,
The sinewy bearers with their cat-like stride,
Dripping with sweat, that merry dark-eyed girl,
Whose sudden beauty shook us from our dreams,
And chained our eyes. How beautiful she was?
Half-hid among the gay Miletian cushions,
The lovely laughing face, the gracious form,
The fragrant lightly-knotted hair, and eyes
Full of the dancing fire of wanton Corinth.
That happy stripling, whose delighted feet
Swung at her side, whose tongue ran on so gaily,
Is it for him alone she wreathes those smiles,
And tunes so musically that flexile voice,
Soft as the Lydian flute? Surely his gait
Proclaimed the lover, and his well-filled girdle
Not less the lover's strength. How joyously
He strode, unmindful of his ruffled curls,
Whose perfumes still went wide upon the wind,
His dust-stained robe unheeded, and the stones
Whose ragged edges frayed his delicate shoes.
How radiant, how full of hope he was!
What pleasant memories, how many things
Rose up again before me, as I lay
Half-stretched among the crushed anemones,
And watched them, till a far off jutting ledge
Precluded sight, still listening till mine ears
Caught the last vanishing murmur of their talk.

Only a little longer; then we rose
With limbs refreshed, and kept a swinging pace
Toward Corinth; but our talk, I know not why,
Fell for that day. I wonder what there was
About those dainty lovers or their speech,
That changed Euktemon's mood; for all the way
From high Cleonæ to the city gates,
Till sunset found us loitering without aim,
Half lost among the dusky-moving crowds,
I could get nothing from him but dark looks,
Short answers and the old defiant stride.
Some memory pricked him. It may be, perchance,
A woman's treachery, some luckless passion,
In former days endured, hath seared his blood,
And dowered him with that cureless bitter humour.

To him solitude and the wanderer's life
Alone are sweet, the tumults of this world
A thing unworthy of the wise man's touch,
Its joys and sorrows to be met alike
With broad-browed scorn. One quality at least
We have in common; we are idlers both,
Shifters and wanderers through this sleepless world,
Albeit in different moods. 'Tis that, I think,
That knit us, and the universal need
For near companionship. Howe'er it be,
There is no hand that I would gladlier grasp,
Either on earth or in the nether gloom,
When the grey keel shall grind the Stygian strand,
Than stern Euktemon's.

II   SONNETS.

Love-Doubt
Yearning upon the faint rose-curves that flit
About her child-sweet mouth and innocent cheek,
And in her eyes watching with eyes all meek
The light and shadow of laughter, I would sit
Mute, knowing our two souls might never knit;
As if a pale proud lily-flower should seek
The love of some red rose, but could not speak
One word of her blithe tongue to tell of it.

For oh, my Love was sunny-lipped and stirred
With all swift light and sound and gloom not long
Retained; I, with dreams weighed, that ever heard
Sad burdens echoing through the loudest throng
She, the wild song of some May-merry bird;
I, but the listening maker of a song.

Perfect Love
Beloved, those who moan of love's brief day
Shall find but little grace with me, I guess,
Who know too well this passion's tenderness
To deem that it shall lightly pass away,
A moment's interlude in life's dull play;
Though many loves have lingered to distress,
So shall not ours, sweet Lady, ne'ertheless,
But deepen with us till both heads be grey.

For perfect love is like a fair green plant,
That fades not with its blossoms, but lives on,
And gentle lovers shall not come to want,
Though fancy with its first mad dream be gone;

Sweet is the flower, whose radiant glory flies,
But sweeter still the green that never dies.

Love-Wonder

Or whether sad or joyous be her hours,
Yet ever is she good and ever fair.
If she be glad, 'tis like a child's wild air,
Who claps her hands above a heap of flowers;
And if she's sad, it is no cloud that lowers,
Rather a saint's pale grace, whose golden hair
Gleams like a crown, whose eyes are like a prayer
From some quiet window under minster towers.

But ah, Beloved, how shall I be taught
To tell this truth in any rhymed line?
For words and woven phrases fall to naught,
Lost in the silence of one dream divine,
Wrapped in the beating wonder of this thought:
Even thou, who art so precious, thou art mine!

Comfort

Comfort the sorrowful with watchful eyes
In silence, for the tongue cannot avail.
Vex not his wounds with rhetoric, nor the stale
Worn truths, that are but maddening mockeries
To him whose grief outmasters all replies.
Only watch near him gently; do but bring
The piteous help of silent ministering,
Watchful and tender. This alone is wise.

So shall thy presence and thine every motion,
The grateful knowledge of thy sad devotion
Melt out the passionate hardness of his grief,
And break the flood-gates of the pent-up soul.
He shall bow down beneath thy mute control,
And take thine hands, and weep, and find relief.

Despondency

Slow figures in some live remorseless frieze,
The approaching days escapeless and unguessed,
With mask and shroud impenetrably dressed;
Time, whose inexorable destinies
Bear down upon us like impending seas;
And the huge presence of this world, at best
A sightless giant wandering without rest,
Agèd and mad with many miseries.

The weight and measure of these things who knows?
Resting at times beside life's thought-swept stream,

Sobered and stunned with unexpected blows,
We scarcely hear the uproar; life doth seem,
Save for the certain nearness of its woes,
Vain and phantasmal as a sick man's dream.

Outlook

Not to be conquered by these headlong days,
But to stand free: to keep the mind at brood
On life's deep meaning, nature's altitude
Of loveliness, and time's mysterious ways;
At every thought and deed to clear the haze
Out of our eyes, considering only this,
What man, what life, what love, what beauty is,
This is to live, and win the final praise.

Though strife, ill fortune and harsh human need
Beat down the soul, at moments blind and dumb
With agony; yet, patience there shall come
Many great voices from life's outer sea,
Hours of strange triumph, and, when few men heed,
Murmurs and glimpses of eternity.

Gentleness

Blind multitudes that jar confusedly
At strife, earth's children, will ye never rest
From toils made hateful here, and dawns distressed
With ravelling self-engendered misery?
And will ye never know, till sleep shall see
Your graves, how dreadful and how dark indeed
Are pride, self-will, and blind-voiced anger, greed,
And malice with its subtle cruelty?

How beautiful is gentleness, whose face
Like April sunshine, or the summer rain,
Swells everywhere the buds of generous thought?
So easy, and so sweet it is; its grace
Smoothes out so soon the tangled knots of pain.
Can ye not learn it? will ye not be taught?

A Prayer

Oh earth, oh dewy mother, breathe on us
Something of all thy beauty and thy might,
Us that are part of day, but most of night,
Not strong like thee, but ever burdened thus
With glooms and cares, things pale and dolorous
Whose gladest moments are not wholly bright;
Something of all thy freshness and thy light,
Oh earth, oh mighty mother, breathe on us.

Oh mother, who wast long before our day,
And after us full many an age shalt be.
Careworn and blind, we wander from thy way:
Born of thy strength, yet weak and halt are we
Grant us, oh mother, therefore, us who pray,
Some little of thy light and majesty.

Music

Move on, light hands, so strongly tenderly,
Now with dropped calm and yearning undersong,
Now swift and loud, tumultuously strong,
And I in darkness, sitting near to thee,
Shall only hear, and feel, but shall not see,
One hour made passionately bright with dreams,
Keen glimpses of life's splendour, dashing gleams
Of what we would, and what we cannot be.

Surely not painful ever, yet not glad,
Shall such hours be to me, but blindly sweet,
Sharp with all yearning and all fact at strife,
Dreams that shine by with unremembered feet,
And tones that like far distance make this life
Spectral and wonderful and strangely sad.

Knowledge

What is more large than knowledge and more sweet;
Knowledge of thoughts and deeds, of rights and wrongs,
Of passions and of beauties and of songs;
Knowledge of life; to feel its great heart beat
Through all the soul upon her crystal seat;
To see, to feel, and evermore to know;
To till the old world's wisdom till it grow
A garden for the wandering of our feet.

Oh for a life of leisure and broad hours,
To think and dream, to put away small things,
This world's perpetual leaguer of dull naughts;
To wander like the bee among the flowers
Till old age find us weary, feet and wings
Grown heavy with the gold of many thoughts.

Sight

The world is bright with beauty, and its days
Are filled with music; could we only know
True ends from false, and lofty things from low;
Could we but tear away the walls that graze
Our very elbows in life's frosty ways;
Behold the width beyond us with its flow,
Its knowledge and its murmur and its glow,

Where doubt itself is but a golden haze.

Ah brothers, still upon our pathway lies
The shadow of dim weariness and fear,
Yet if we could but lift our earthward eyes
To see, and open our dull ears to hear,
Then should the wonder of this world draw near
And life's innumerable harmonies.

An Old Lesson From The Fields

Even as I watched the daylight how it sped
From noon till eve, and saw the light wind pass
In long pale waves across the flashing grass,
And heard through all my dreams, wherever led,
The thin cicada singing overhead,
I felt what joyance all this nature has,
And saw myself made clear as in a glass,
How that my soul was for the most part dead.

Oh, light, I cried, and, heaven, with all your blue,
Oh, earth, with all your sunny fruitfulness,
And ye, tall lilies, of the wind-vexed field,
What power and beauty life indeed might yield,
Could we but cast away its conscious stress,
Simple of heart, becoming even as you.

Winter-Thought

The wind-swayed daisies, that on every side
Throng the wide fields in whispering companies,
Serene and gently smiling like the eyes
Of tender children long beatified,
The delicate thought-wrapped buttercups that glide
Like sparks of fire above the wavering grass,
And swing and toss with all the airs that pass,
Yet seem so peaceful, so preoccupied;

These are the emblems of pure pleasures flown,
I scarce can think of pleasure without these.
Even to dream of them is to disown
The cold forlorn midwinter reveries,
Lulled with the perfume of old hopes new-blown,
No longer dreams, but dear realities.

Deeds

'Tis well with words, oh masters, ye have sought
To turn men's yearning to the great and true,
Yet first take heed to what your own hands do;
By deeds not words the souls of men are taught;
Good lives alone are fruitful; they are caught

Into the fountain of all life (wherethrough
Men's souls that drink are broken or made new)
Like drops of heavenly elixir, fraught
With the clear essence of eternal youth.
Even one little deed of weak untruth
Is like a drop of quenchless venom cast,
A liquid thread, into life's feeding stream,
Woven forever with its crystal gleam,
Bearing the seed of death and woe at last.

Aspiration

Oh deep-eyed brothers was there ever here,
Or is there now, or shall there sometime be
Harbour or any rest for such as we,
Lone thin-cheeked mariners, that aye must steer
Our whispering barks with such keen hope and fear
Toward misty bournes across that coastless sea,
Whose winds are songs that ever gust and flee,
Whose shores are dreams that tower but come not near.

Yet we perchance, for all that flesh and mind
Of many ills be marked with many a trace,
Shall find this life more sweet more strangely kind,
Than they of that dim-hearted earthly race,
Who creep firm-nailed upon the earth's hard face,
And hear nor see not, being deaf and blind.

The Poets

Half god, half brute, within the self-same shell,
Changers with every hour from dawn till even,
Who dream with angels in the gate of heaven,
And skirt with curious eyes the brinks of hell,
Children of Pan, whom some, the few, love well,
But most draw back, and know not what to say,
Poor shining angels, whom the hoofs betray,
Whose pinions frighten with their goatish smell.

Half brutish, half divine, but all of earth,
Half-way 'twixt hell and heaven, near to man,
The whole world's tangle gathered in one span,
Full of this human torture and this mirth:
Life with its hope and error, toil and bliss,
Earth-born, earth-reared, ye know it as it is.

The Truth

Friend, though thy soul should burn thee, yet be still.
Thoughts were not meant for strife, nor tongues for swords.
He that sees clear is gentlest of his words,
And that's not truth that hath the heart to kill.

The whole world's thought shall not one truth fulfil.
Dull in our age, and passionate in youth,
No mind of man hath found the perfect truth,
Nor shalt thou find it; therefore, friend, be still.

Watch and be still, nor hearken to the fool,
The babbler of consistency and rule:
Wisest is he, who, never quite secure,
Changes his thoughts for better day by day:
To-morrow some new light will shine, be sure,
And thou shalt see thy thought another way.

The Martyrs

Oh ye, who found in men's brief ways no sign
Of strength or help, so cast them forth, and threw
Your whole souls up to one ye deemed most true,
Nor failed nor doubted but held fast your line,
Seeing before you that divine face shine;
Shall we not mourn, when yours are now so few,
Those sterner days, when all men yearned to you,
White souls whose beauty made their world divine:

Yet still across life's tangled storms we see,
Following the cross, your pale procession led,
One hope, one end, all others sacrificed,
Self-abnegation, love, humility,
Your faces shining toward the bended head,
The wounded hands and patient feet of Christ.

A Night Of Storm

Oh city, whom grey stormy hands have sown
With restless drift, scarce broken now of any,
Out of the dark thy windows dim and many
Gleam red across the storm. Sound is there none,
Save evermore the fierce wind's sweep and moan,
From whose grey hands the keen white snow is shaken
In desperate gusts, that fitfully lull and waken,
Dense as night's darkness round thy towers of stone.

Darkling and strange art thou thus vexed and chidden;
More dark and strange thy veilèd agony,
City of storm, in whose grey heart are hidden
What stormier woes, what lives that groan and beat,
Stern and thin-cheeked, against time's heavier sleet,
Rude fates, hard hearts, and prisoning poverty.

The Railway Station

The darkness brings no quiet here, the light
No waking: ever on my blinded brain

The flare of lights, the rush, and cry, and strain,
The engines' scream, the hiss and thunder smite:
I see the hurrying crowds, the clasp, the flight,
Faces that touch, eyes that are dim with pain:
I see the hoarse wheels turn, and the great train
Move labouring out into the bourneless night.

So many souls within its dim recesses,
So many bright, so many mournful eyes:
Mine eyes that watch grow fixed with dreams and guesses;
What threads of life, what hidden histories,
What sweet or passionate dreams and dark distresses,
What unknown thoughts, what various agonies!

A Forecast

What days await this woman, whose strange feet
Breathe spells, whose presence makes men dream like wine,
Tall, free and slender as the forest pine,
Whose form is moulded music, through whose sweet
Frank eyes I feel the very heart's least beat,
Keen, passionate, full of dreams and fire:
How in the end, and to what man's desire
Shall all this yield, whose lips shall these lips meet?

One thing I know: if he be great and pure,
This love, this fire, this beauty shall endure;
Triumph and hope shall lead him by the palm:
But if not this, some differing thing he be,
That dream shall break in terror; he shall see
The whirlwind ripen, where he sowed the calm.

In November

The hills and leafless forests slowly yield
To the thick-driving snow. A little while
And night shall darken down. In shouting file
The woodmen's carts go by me homeward-wheeled,
Past the thin fading stubbles, half concealed,
Now golden-grey, sowed softly through with snow,
Where the last ploughman follows still his row,
Turning black furrows through the whitening field.

Far off the village lamps begin to gleam,
Fast drives the snow, and no man comes this way;
The hills grow wintery white, and bleak winds moan
About the naked uplands. I alone
Am neither sad, nor shelterless, nor grey,
Wrapped round with thought, content to watch and dream.

The City

Beyond the dusky corn-fields, toward the west,
Dotted with farms, beyond the shallow stream,
Through drifts of elm with quiet peep and gleam,
Curved white and slender as a lady's wrist,
Faint and far off out of the autumn mist,
Even as a pointed jewel softly set
In clouds of colour warmer, deeper yet,
Crimson and gold and rose and amethyst,
Toward dayset, where the journeying sun grown old
Hangs lowly westward darker now than gold,
With the soft sun-touch of the yellowing hours
Made lovelier, I see with dreaming eyes,
Even as a dream out of a dream, arise
The bell-tongued city with its glorious towers.

Midsummer Night

Mother of balms and soothings manifold,
Quiet-breathèd night whose brooding hours are seven,
To whom the voices of all rest are given,
And those few stars whose scattered names are told,
Far off beyond the westward hills outrolled,
Darker than thou, more still, more dreamy even,
The golden moon leans in the dusky heaven,
And under her one star - a point of gold:

And all go slowly lingering toward the west,
As we go down forgetfully to our rest,
Weary of daytime, tired of noise and light:
Ah, it was time that thou should'st come; for we
Were sore athirst, and had great need of thee,
Thou sweet physician, balmy-bosomed night.

The Loons

Once ye were happy, once by many a shore,
Wherever Glooscap's gentle feet might stray,
Lulled by his presence like a dream, ye lay
Floating at rest; but that was long of yore.
He was too good for earthly men; he bore
Their bitter deeds for many a patient day,
And then at last he took his unseen way.
He was your friend, and ye might rest no more:

And now, though many hundred altering years
Have passed, among the desolate northern meres
Still must ye search and wander querulously,
Crying for Glooscap, still bemoan the light
With wierd entreaties, and in agony
With awful laughter pierce the lonely night.

March

Over the dripping roofs and sunk snow-barrows
The bells are ringing loud and strangely near,
The shout of children dins upon mine ear
Shrilly, and like a flight of silvery arrows
Showers the sweet gossip of the British sparrows,
Gathered in noisy knots of one or two,
To joke and chatter just as mortals do
Over the days long tale of joys and sorrows;

Talk before bed-time of bold deeds together
Of thefts and fights, of hard-times and the weather,
Till sleep disarm them, to each little brain
Bringing tucked wings and many a blissful dream,
Visions of wind and sun, of field and stream,
And busy barn-yards with their scattered grain.

Solitude

How still it is here in the woods. The trees
Stand motionless, as if they did not dare
To stir, lest it should break the spell. The air
Hangs quiet as spaces in a marble frieze.
Even this little brook, that runs at ease,
Whispering and gurgling in its knotted bed,
Seems but to deepen with its curling thread
Of sound the shadowy sun-pierced silences.

Sometimes a hawk screams or a woodpecker
Startles the stillness from its fixèd mood
With his loud careless tap. Sometimes I hear
The dreamy white-throat from some far off tree
Pipe slowly on the listening solitude
His five pure notes succeeding pensively.

Autumn Maples

The thoughts of all the maples who shall name,
When the sad landscape turns to cold and grey?
Yet some for very ruth and sheer dismay,
Hearing the northwind pipe the winter's name,
Have fired the hills with beaconing clouds of flame;
And some with softer woe that day by day,
So sweet and brief, should go the westward way,
Have yearned upon the sunset with such shame,

That all their cheeks have turned to tremulous rose;
Others for wrath have turned a rusty red,
And some that knew not either grief or dread,
Ere the old year should find its iron close,
Have gathered down the sun's last smiles acold,
Deep, deep, into their luminous hearts of gold.

The Dog

"Grotesque!" we said, the moment we espied him,
For there he stood, supreme in his conceit,
With short ears close together and queer feet
Planted irregularly: first we tried him
With jokes, but they were lost; we then defied him
With bantering questions and loose criticism:
He did not like, I'm sure, our catechism,
But whisked and snuffed a little as we eyed him.

Then flung we balls, and out and clear away,
Up the white slope, across the crusted snow,
To where a broken fence stands in the way,
Against the sky-line, a mere row of pegs,
Quicker than thought we saw him flash and go,
A straight mad scuttling of four crooked legs.

www.ingramcontent.com/pod-product-compliance
Lightning Source LLC
Chambersburg PA
CBHW060145050426
42448CB00010B/2299